MY IRELAND

BY

LORD DUNSANY

ILLUSTRATED

British Library Cataloguing-in-Publication Data
A catalogue record for this book is available from the
British Library

Lord Dunsany

Lord Dunsany was born Edward John Moreton Drax
Plunkett in London in 1878. Dunsany's youth was spent in
Dunsany, Ireland – his family home – and Kent. He
attended school at Cheam and Eton, before entering the
Royal Military Academy Sandhurst in 1896. He inherited his
father's title shortly before fighting in the Second Anglo-
Boer War between 1899 and 1901. Dunsany published his
first book a collection of Anglo-Irish fantasy stories entitled
The Gods of Pegana, in 1905.

Over the course of his life, Dunsany was a prolific writer,
penning short stories, novels, plays, poetry, essays and
autobiography. During the peak of his career he was
something of a literary celebrity, spending time with authors
such as W. B. Yeats and Rudyard Kipling. He published over
sixty books, and his plays were highly successful; at one
point, five Dunsany works were running simultaneously in
New York. His most notable fantasy short stories were
published between 1905 and 1919, in collections such as *The
Sword of Welleran and Other Stories* (1908), *A Dreamer's*

Tales (1910), *The Book of Wonder* (1912) and *Tales of Wonder* (1916). Amongst his best-regarded novels are *Don Rodriguez: Chronicles of Shadow Valley* (1922), *The King of Elfland's Daughter* (1924), and *The Charwoman's Shadow* (1926).

Dunsany died in old age, following an attack of appendicitis. Over the course of his writing life, he greatly influenced a wide range of authors. Arthur C. Clarke called him "one of the greatest writers of [the 20th] century," and H. P. Lovecraft described him as being "unexcelled in the sorcery of crystalline singing prose, and supreme in the creation of a gorgeous and languorous world of incandescently exotic vision."

Contents

v

CONTENTS

Illustrations

I

A. E.

IF I let myself be lured to attempt to distil a story
from so wide an area as Ireland, it seems to me
that I should somehow get some clear view of it.
How shall I get that? Shall it be by motoring over
every road in Ireland? I think not: the material
would be too much for use, and I should see so
much that was new to me, and so see it almost as a
stranger. I will rather look again at fields and
streams that I know, and the view of them may
strengthen and brighten my memories, and so I
shall tell of the Ireland that I know best. And
whence shall I see most of it? Fortunately the spot
from which one can see most of Ireland is a field
that stands in the center of Irish history, and is but
a few hundred yards from the edge of my own
land. It is Tara. So there I will go.

When I came to Tara and looked over the plain
of Meath there was a storm like a little lost thing,
in the west, going before a south wind with the
sunlight chasing it. Green fields turned silvery
under it as it came. The skirts of the rain went
before it, and intensely bright fields flashed where
the storm had not yet come. It shadowed a county,

with silvery-green parishes standing out clear here and there, and went away to the north, where hills were gleaming in sunlight; for storms over this plain seem to pass like travelers, like dark men walking rarely along a wide road that forgets them. Far off, like happy ghosts, the Dublin Mountains smiled where the passing shafts of sunlight touched them. They sit and smile at one end of that panorama, which goes from them in the south round by Slieve Bloom and the Hill of Usnagh, past all the hills beyond Oldcastle, to where the Mourne Mountains looking upon the sea end the great view away in the northeast.

So let me begin my memories at the feet of those mountains that give a continual surprise and beauty to Dublin; for you suddenly catch a sight of them looking down the end of a street, and their wild and lovely heads whenever seen seem something you did not expect to see from a city. Much has been lost to Dublin in my time, for instance the Four Courts and the Customs House. And though the Customs House has been rebuilt, and most of the Four Courts, yet they both seem to me dead. I had this feeling only the other day as I passed the Four Courts; the feeling was so strong that I knew that I must have seen something that made this certain, but my intellect was not quick enough to make out what it was. All I could notice was that the great coats of arms with their life-sized supporters were shattered, but beyond them the buildings had the air of repaired ruins, with all their windows neatly filled with glass. They are still standing there, while A. E. is dead; and yet when my memories revisit Dublin the presence of A. E. appears so vivid that it seems as though he still lived or his work were immortal. To tell of the Ireland I know, without telling something of that rare spirit produced by it, would be like telling of Irish fields and forgetting the shamrock. He edited an agricultural paper in a room at the top of a house in Merrion Square. And there he worked all day. Over a large desk, heaped with untidiness, a window shone, and through the window a glimpse of the Dublin Mountains.

All round the dingy room A. E. had gone with his brush, making a fairyland from floor to ceiling. Figures with plumes and aureoles over their heads walked there in glades a little too bright for this earth, but helping perhaps to mitigate for A. E. the tedium of agricultural economics and making the average of his surroundings tolerable for him. But, for all that, I never saw him at his work without a certain memory of Las Palmas when, young and full of the romance of the camel and the deserts that he roved, I saw him harnessed to a roller. "He is doing a hundred times more useful work where he is than he would be by writing poetry," said the owner of A. E.'s roller. But one man in every thousand could have done the economics for that agricultural paper quite as well as A. E. did; while if among the four million in Ireland there is now one who can do A. E.'s other work, I shall be very glad to hear of him, but doubtful of the news; though I hope that within a hundred years there may be such another.

Nor is there any comparison between the good that a man may do to his fellows by teaching them sound business principles (if business has principles), and on the other hand by telling them something of the spirit and what it has seen on the way. The upholders of the first kind of work always win their shallow arguments by showing precisely in pounds, shillings and pence just what is the gain to man, while the upholders of the other kind know that here is a value that pounds and shillings and pence are all three of them equally unable to estimate. We do not even know the price of a dawn.

The above remarks may throw some light on the strange circumstance that, although there is a depth in A. E.'s thought and a melody in its expression that is worthy of a great poet, yet the quantity of his work is rather that of a poet who had died young, than of one who had attained as he did to the years of the psalmist. Of the quality of those lovely lyrics Posterity will judge; and I believe we are right in supposing that Posterity judges unerringly; but Posterity would be saved a good deal

of time in making up its mind if it could have the
advantage that I have had, of hearing A. E. read
his own poems himself. The sonorous melody that
was at all times in his voice rose then to its full
splendor; so that there was the difference between
reading his verse and hearing him read it, that
there is between reading music and hearing it from
an organ. Not that there is an essential difference;
for music can ring in a musician's imagination as
clearly as down the aisles, and poetry, to those that
care for it, should give all its aroma from the
printed page; but it certainly saved trouble to hear
it thus, and enabled one to be sure, without any
strain on one's intellect, that this was great poetry.
Alas that it was so scant. A heavy stone flies
further than a light one. And yet if the light one
that is thrown be a diamond, may not the brilliance
of its flash be seen beyond the distance that its
heavier rival can travel? And so A. E.'s slender
books may come to a far posterity.

Perhaps in writing of this remarkable Irishman
it is least necessary for me to write of his poetry,
for that is printed for all the world to see, and it
would be far better to buy one of A. E.'s books
than to read what I have to say of them, as it is
better to read any poetry in the world than any
commentator upon it; but I should say something
of his mind, as I came to know it through many
conversations. It seemed as though he were always

looking back down the ages eastwards, in the direction from which the Irish people are said to have come. Indeed in this one man's mind I should look for evidence of that old journey as readily as in a page of history. There would come an eager look in his blue eyes and bearded face, such as one might compare to the look on the face of a child seeing jam through a window; through the dim ages he would peer thus at some old Indian philosophy, and speak of the things of the spirit as though they were nearer to us than any material thing. I was once speaking of A. E. at a public meeting, and I mentioned the strange orientalism of his outlook, and his philosophy that was strange in a man who had never been to India. My chairman, Mr. Robin Flower, speaking afterwards, said that A. E. had himself told him that he had been to India. The audience pricked up its ears at this conflict of opinion between chairman and speaker; and well it might, for it heard a most remarkable story. A. E. had told Mr. Flower that he was once walking in Ireland past a row of poplars standing at regular intervals, and as he passed the second poplar his soul suddenly left his body and flew to India. There it entered the body of a child, and dwelt there, and lived in an Indian village. His memory of that village was very clear; he spent his life there. He grew to manhood in that village; and then one day some tribe from beyond the village

went to war with it, and in the fighting A. E. was
killed. His soul returned to his body, and A. E.
noticed at the end of that life's story that he was
just walking past the third poplar tree.

But there is another part of A. E.'s mind that I
must not forget, for any account of him that neglected it would be very deficient; and that is his
generosity. To young poets he would give en-
couragement straight from the spirit, which he
himself valued so much more than gold. There
are, I suppose, various ways of writing poetry, but
what A. E. wrote was poetry because he himself
was a poet and whatever came from that great-
hearted source was poetry, as what comes from
springs is water. Besides the room at the top of
the house with a view of the Dublin Mountains, in
which A. E., helped by Miss Susan Mitchell, herself a poet, brought out of a heap of untidiness,
which as he once told me gave a touch of Chaos
to his writing-table, the agricultural paper, he was
also to be seen in his house in Rathgar Avenue,
where on Sunday evenings he always had a reception for such as cared to come, mostly poets. It was
there that I first met James Stephens, a man soon
to make a name as great as A. E.'s, but then excited
by the approaching appearance of his first book,
and telling us how he would stand still and gaze
into the window of the bookshop when he saw his
book there, and yet not believing that such an event

would ever come to pass; thinking rather that Fate
would let him live until a day or two before the
book was to appear in that window and would then
snatch everything away from him. Events showed
that he misjudged Fate, but I do think that all the
rest that he said on that occasion showed a very
proper spirit of a worker towards his work. And
as Puck found a patron in Oberon, so with this very
similar pair James Stephens found help and en-
couragement from A. E., until he no longer needed
them.

I mention lastly A. E.'s pictures; lastly because,
although they mirrored A. E.'s mind and the splendid plumed figures that walked there, and although
they captured Irish evenings, their colored twi-
lights touched to a deeper radiance by A. E.'s imagination, yet the actual work of his brush had not
the supreme artistry of his pen; the same vision of
mystery and evening and Ireland when expressed
by him in melody must, I think, be more enduring
than what he was able to express of it upon canvas.
He was so Irish in his poetry and in his love of the
hills and streams of Ireland, and even in his Oriental air, that we may hope that some man something
like him may one of these days be found in Ireland
again; but not in my time; and, even if there were,
he would not to me be compensation for the loss of
those eyes that seemed to peer, far from the dingy

room that he made less dingy, past books upon economics, past even the Dublin Mountains, to catch flashes and glimpses of what his strange spirit knew were the things that really mattered.

II

Tara

Let us go back to Tara, whither all the races
came that conquered Ireland, and where their
kings ruled, dynasty after dynasty, until they were
driven thence by a strange thing; for neither the
sword nor sickness, nor any material power, de-
prived the hill of its government: it was a curse of
the priests that turned the halls of Tara into long
mounds and that brought the grass up over all of
them.   Here came the earliest people of whom
Irish history knows, and three races after them before the Normans, and all came to Tara.   Did they
see Tara rising up like music, an inspiration to
those early kings?   Or was it only the ideal place
for cattle, a wider field for them than the neighboring height of Skryne, the best grass in Europe,
and a view that enabled sentries to see the approach of any enemy with a taste for beef, for a
long time before he could reach them from any
direction?

And, besides being the ideal place for feeding
and guarding cattle, Tara shared with most of the
capitals of the world a position that seems almost
a requisite for the capital of a people that are to

make any name in history: it is about twenty miles from the sea. Of course the distance varies among capitals; but hardly any of them are on the coast, for they would have been too tempting to pirates, and would never have survived infancy; and they are seldom far from the sea, for they could take no great part, if they were, in the affairs of the world. Tara, however, had not all the requisites of a great capital, for it had no river to link it up with the sea. Had Rome, London, or Paris been without their rivers, or Constantinople without its inlet, other histories would have to have been written than those we read. Their water they got at Tara from a spring, below the top of the hill on the eastern side, and it is a holy well to this day. Nearly all such springs in Ireland are holy: the mystery of them, their brightness and their value, probably appealed to the Irish people, who have so much mystery in their story; and they dedicated them to their gods. Later there came the saints; and, when Ireland was converted to Christianity, these wells remained as reminders that the people had not always been quite so civilized. So the priests, who could not stop the wells being holy, picketed each one with a saint, and now they are St. John's well and St. James's well and St. Peter's well that are dotted about the country.

When I came to Tara, lines of pale clouds, like the ghosts of kings, were passing over the hill as

I came up to it. They were far in the west; to the northeast the Mourne Mountains, like a family of giants out for a walk in the evening, were clearer in the fading light of evening than they are ever seen in broad day, while a hundred miles away from these the peaks of the Slieve Bloom lifting from King's County made a shadow upon the sky no darker than clouds, and hardly to be distinguished from them. In the south the Dublin Mountains were still smiling. All these things the earliest men to come to Tara would have seen, standing where I stood; changing as mountains change, hourly; and yet suggesting to every mind that ever sees mountains a scale of permanence that our years and our days and our hours have no power to measure.

The race of which history first knows in Ireland, came from the far end of Europe, and whence that wandering people came before that none knows. They came to land in sight of Tara under the Dublin Mountains, and called it Moy Elta, the Plain of the Flocks of Birds, and there they dwelt for a while till they were all killed by the plague. They all died in one week on the Plain of the Flocks of Birds. And that was before the coming of the Firbolgs.

When the only race of which history seems to know in that time in Ireland was all dead, what remained? Was it only the Irish elk, the wolf, the fox, the wild boar and the hare, before the Firbolgs came? Or was there some other race of men, of whom history does not tell? As history is silent we turn to legend. And there is abundant evidence of an earlier race than any we know today, and in all probability earlier than the Firbolgs. Who are the people that come out at evening to dance on the raths, the folk to whom old thorns are sacred? No age has been without tales of them, and the reign of King George VI is no exception; only they must be asked after very carefully, or the answer will be that no such folk have been seen. I think that they must actually have been there, and that they survived many conquests. There is a ring of truth about the dance round the raths; for those green mounds were hollow; there are several within sight of Tara into which you can crawl to this day; and in these raths the defeated race may have lived where eviction was almost impossible, coming out for exercise at night and sometimes dimly seen just before twilight hid them. After the last of them died, the fear of the small shapes of an injured race furtive and dim in the dusk may have lingered on for ages, until mothers warning their children against the little people may have begun to lose their own fear of them, and yet handed a fear on. And so a memory of them haunts the Irish twilight to this day, and few will willingly dig into a rath or cut down an old thorn.

And then, says legend, the Nemedians came, from Scythia, and were harassed by northern pirates, who harassed them still after they had landed in Ireland. And after many battles one ship's crew of the Nemedians fled and came to Greece, and were the ancestors, so legend tells, of the Firbolgs; who centuries later escaped from some oppression in Greece, and settled in Ireland and held it thirty-six years, when they were defeated by the Dedannaans. This people's burial grounds lie under the hills that one sees to the north of Tara, low hills rising and dipping; with the shoulder of a mountain seen wherever they dip, like a giant stooping beyond them: under them flows the Boyne, and along its banks are the mounds of the Dedannaans.

And in their turn the Dedannaans became a myth, to be told of as fairies, and the Milesians ruled in their country; coming, they say, from Scythia and traveling slowly, so many hundred miles in a generation, and looking for the Isle of Destiny. The fight of which legend tells between the Milesians and the Dedannaans appears to have been a fight of sword against magic, the Dedannaans relying mainly on magic; but, whatever happened, the Milesians came to Tara and thence ruled all Ireland.

And in the Milesians' time legend merges into history, till one comes on authentic names, and

TARA   15

battles that none doubts; and one does not read that
earliest history long before one sees that none of
the disputes of our time are new. About the year
100 the Milesians were asked what they were doing
in those parts, oppressing the people of the country; and many of them were murdered. For a
while after that the Milesian kings were in exile;
until their monarchy was restored under Tuathal,
who extended the estate of the High King of Ireland, from being only the land that lay round Tara,
to be the whole of Meath. Looking from Tara one
sees a pale blue mountain, far beyond Trim and to
the left of the line of it; to the right of the Slieve
Bloom Mountains, that is to say to the north of
them. This pale blue sapphire set in the western
sky is the Hill of Usnagh, lying beyond Eden-
derry; and on it there was a stone, and is to this day,
called the Stone of the Divisions, where all the four
provinces of Ireland met; and round this stone
Tuathal cut out the new province for himself, the
province of Meath, taking a bit from all four.
Tuathal also imposed a tribute upon the Kings of
Leinster, but could seldom draw his rents without
a battle.

In the year 177, Conn was King of Tara, and he
had a great taste for fighting. And the King of
Munster had an equal taste for it, so they made
history and legend, between them, for a great many
years. And Conn became known as Conn of the

Hundred Battles; but, when he had lost ten of them, he agreed to divide Ireland with Owen More, King of Munster, and they chose a line of low steep sandhills running across Ireland, as their boundary. These sandhills are so small and steep that they almost look artificial, as though an army had thrown up a great rampart; and certainly a better line of defense could hardly be made, and no doubt armies recognized this and held it when they came to it, so that it was a very likely line to be chosen to be a frontier.

And yet the steep rampart is not artificial, but was made by glaciers, going through Ireland with their noses down in the soil, like pigs looking for truffles, and grinding the rocks as they went; and then, when the world's axis turned more to the sun again and they melted, all the ground rock that had lain as sand on their backs lay in a long heap where the edge of the iceberg had been. These hills are called eskers among geologists all over the world; and esker is the one word that the Irish language has given to science. It is a wobble in Earth's axis that brings these glaciers, and that shifts the arctic circle nearly as far south as Paris, when the northern end of the axis is furthest away from the sun; which they say occurs once every fifty thousand years.

I know some miles of those sandhills well; they cross all the roads running south from Tara, and only a few miles away from it; sometimes they are

A THATCHED COTTAGE, TYPICAL RURAL IRISH HOME

AN ANCIENT PEAT BOG, IRELAND'S SUBSTITUTE FOR A COAL MINE.

bare; sometimes pine trees stand along them, as though trees had gone to war and the pines were holding the high ground against willows or whatever dwells in the marsh; and sometimes they are covered with gorse, as between Trim and Galtrim, and then they make fine fox-coverts, and the sandy heights have people standing along them when we draw the gorse with the Meath, as eager to see all that they can of the hunt, as no doubt their forbears were to see all they could of the battle, whenever Conn and Owen More came to loggerheads, as they very soon did again; and this time Owen More was killed, and the frontier must have lost its importance, to become in course of time a historical feature, and then an object of interest to geologists, and in many places quarries for sand.

Conn was succeeded by his son Connary, and he by Cormac Mac Art. A hundred years later Niall of the Nine Hostages reigned, the ancestor of the O'Neills, and that brings us to the end of the fourth century. Looking once westwards from Tara, I saw before me rows and rows of trees, thin dark lines with the mist in layers between them; and I thought how history was like that, a sentence or two of fact, and mystery thickly in between the lines. A few trees at the edge of the hill were sighing mournfully, and the wind that troubled them seemed to bring the evening on, for soon the mist had hidden the whole scene, like Time effacing history.

III

St. Patrick

IF we stand on Tara with our backs to the Dublin Mountains, and the white spire of the cathedral in Trim rising up in the west on our left, we are looking northward to a line of low hills not very far away; and one of those hills is Slane. It is the year 433 that I wish to tell of, and Easter eve, when King Laegaire was holding a festival at Tara. We cannot see quite what he saw, for the country was more thickly wooded then, and the hill of Slane will probably be dark; but though we look in the wrong century and even at the wrong time of year, Slane and its woods still stand in sight of us looking from Tara as they stood when Laegaire looked. Let us look, then, from Tara as I did one August day fifteen hundred and three years late, using the outward eye, which does not always see as clear as the eye of imagination; but at least we are standing where Laegaire stood and looking the same way. Huge figures of storm are trailing and striding towards a pale blue mountain far in the southwest, which must be the Hill of Usnagh.

And again and again one sees those stormy shapes on the huge circle of the view. There they are drawing curtains across another mountain, and there they are shrouding far woods. A cornfield shines like a picture on a dark wall. A night-like shower, reaching down from a cloud, has hidden the far mountain. Bright clouds appear in the west and begin to be colored, so that you can understand people imagining Heaven from here, or an earlier people picturing Tirnan-Og, which was still King Laegaire's Heaven. It grows brighter. As fingers of storm darken fields, slanting fingers of light illuminate other fields or pick out steeples, or irradiate a lazy cloud of smoke. The mountains more to the north seem to know nothing of all the darkness that, bedecked with one or two gleaming fields, covers all the west. And now the somber frown of the wood of Fahan is lit with ruby. And now one sees through the darkness hiding Meath, to where in the west there is no storm at all. The mountains there are small and pale blue, as the mountains of Fairyland might be; due north they are deep indigo, while away northeastwards the Mournes stand far aloof, a bluish gray above, and so pale a blue below as almost to be severed from earth by invisible air. To the left of them, and nearer than they, stands the hill of Slane.

Night comes on quietly, with very few lights twinkling out in the plain, and none at all when Laegaire looked, for he was about to light a fire to gods of his, and he had a law that no one at this

time might make any other light. And then a flame
shot up from the top of the hill of Slane fifteen hundred and three years ago, and it was St.
Patrick lighting his paschal fire.   The King's
druids on Tara were naturally against that fire, and
against St. Patrick when he appeared at Tara next
day; but were I to go back all those years to write
of religious animosities in Ireland, like a man leaving Newcastle to look for coal, I might be taken
to task by critics for neglecting our own time. Suffice it to say that the King's chief poet first accepted
the new faith, and helped St. Patrick to preach it;
and the druids probably said, although it had very
likely been said before, "You can never be sure
that a poet will be quite sound in religion."

So St. Patrick went from Tara, unhindered by
the High King, although he had not converted
him, and went westwards preaching and spreading
the Christian faith.   So that, as we stand on Tara,
we look over land that knew Christianity when in
most other lands there were still being worshiped
gods against whom I do not wish to say anything
critical, but who certainly had a liking for human
sacrifice (if their priests understood their wishes),
a custom with which since the teaching of Patrick
no Irishmen have had anything to do—for any
Cause except politics.

For a hundred and thirty more years after St.
Patrick came, Tara remained the seat of the Irish

kings; and then came the conflict, that other countries besides Ireland have known, between the Government and the power of the priests. And the
priests won, for they intrigued against Tara, or,
as legend tells us, they cursed it; and the kings left
Tara, and the halls of Tara fell, and nothing now
remains to mark the home of so many dynasties but
long green ridges showing the great length of the
hall, and burial mounds and one ancient stone.
The stone is thought by some to be the Stone of
Destiny, the Lia Fail of which legend speaks.
That it is ancient is obvious, being of pre-Christian
shape; but it seems to me unlikely to be the Lia
Fail, because it is told that the kings were crowned
standing upon that stone, and you could not stand
upon this stone unless you happened to be a bird.
Who walk round it to this day I do not know; and
that, I should say, you are not likely to see; but
certainly the stone retains some ancient reputation,
for the grass all round it is trodden, and evidently
many people walk carefully round it. I was looking at this one day when a man came by with a dog,
and I knew from the look of the dog that the man
was a herder, but not the herder of those fields; he
was walking too fast for that, and he turned out
to be a man coming up the hill from the west,
looking for a goat that had strayed. The goat had
come to fields of the man that employed him two
or three years before, and he had thought it lucky,

for it is held to be lucky if a goat comes to dwell in your field, but now it was off to make some other farmer lucky and the herder was after it. This man, I thought, will know a lot more about Ireland than I do, so I got into conversation with him, and standing there upon Tara he became very national. "The country doesn't rightly belong to the Normans," he said, "for they took it from the Milesians."

"They shouldn't have done that," I said.

"Sure, it served them right," said he; "for didn't they take it from the Tuatha de Danaan?"

"That was a shame," I said.

"It was not," said he, "for it only served them right, for they took it away from the Firbolgs."

"Then the Firbolgs ought to have it now," I said.

"Ah," he said, "they should not, for they'd only be killing all them Dublin boys that have got it now, for taking the country away from them."

"Wouldn't that be a pity?" I asked, trying to get at his politics.

And he thought for awhile. "Begob it might," he said, "for maybe we shouldn't be getting any more free beef then."

"Free beef is a fine thing," I said.

"There's nothing finer," he answered, "only one thing."

And somehow I saw from a yearning look in his eyes what that thing was.

"Would you like to come as far as my car?" I said. "I have a small flask of whisky in it."

"The light of Heaven to you in the next world," he said, "and glory and riches in this."

As that whisky went down, the evening was descending on Tara. There had been bright sun all day, but now the haze was shutting out all the hills; within the circle of it lay the fields that are the daily concern of those that till or graze them; beyond it the hills lay unseen, like myth beyond history. And I thought what a store and treasure of myth that man would have in his mind; but I did not ask him about it, any more than one troubles bankers to tell you how much money they have, still less to give you some of it: had I asked him straight out about the Fairy People he would probably have disowned them, and we should both of us have felt awkward. When I think how small the country is, and how much inbred are the people, I think the chances are hundreds to one that he is descended from many of the kings and their druids who knew the hall of Tara before they fell out with the priests.

We talked a little more of Milesians and Firbolgs; but I do not write what he told me here, as it is at variance with things I have written already, as is often the case with legend, whence comes a pleasing variety. And then he walked away by the way he had come, over the field going west-wards, as though he had forgotten his quest.

"Are you giving up your search?" I asked.

"Ah, isn't it only a bloody old goat," he called back to me, and walked on fully content, as though the thought of the Firbolgs was amply sufficient for him.

Then shafts of late sunlight took a last look at the plain, with long shadows amongst them, giving beauty and mystery to what was left of the view, and a touch of the sinister; as though profusion of blessings and curses were poured on the limestone plateau. For a moment I was awed and charmed by the sight of it; when it suddenly struck me that, in this book that I am planning to write about Ireland, there is only one thing that anyone will want to hear, a thing without which the book will be totally uninstructive, and that is—What the people of Ireland actually think of the new form of government.

Whom should I ask about this? I wanted some fairly representative man. Whom should I choose? And, standing there on Tara, it suddenly struck me that in the characters of fiction there is a certain blending of human traits that is a little more in-tense than what you usually find amongst men who cast shadows; also such people are always there when you want them, whereas the others may happen to be out when you go to see them, having gone to stop a bit of a gap in a hedge, or being over beyond in a neighboring village, where they have gone to see a man about a dog; or, worst of all, they may be dead. So I decided that it was of a character of fiction that I would inquire; and, happening to know fairly well one that was called Old Mickey, I decided that he was the man for this essential information.

I would go to Old Mickey.

IV

Old Mickey

So to Old Mickey I went; and found him where he always sat, in a wooden chair in his doorway, watching the affairs of Cranogue, a village lying hid in the haze and distance that surrounds the lands you can clearly see from Tara.

"And how's the general?" was the first question I asked him, partly because one does not go straight to the point, whatever one's business, in Ireland.

Young Mickey, the old man's grandson, had taken a prominent part in a war that there was in the hills, leading a band of eight men, nine including the general himself, and later he had joined the Irish Guards. It was to him I alluded.

"Ah, he'll not speak to me now," said the old man.

Yet there was a certain pride in his voice, so that I continued to talk of Young Mickey in spite of the old man's words.

"Why is that?" I asked.

"Sure he's too grand," said Old Mickey. "They've made him a lance-corporal."

"That was a great promotion," I said.

"Sure, it was," said the old man.

"And he's been having some leave?" I said.

"He has," said Old Mickey, "and making a glory in the street with his fine uniform."

"Did it look well on him?" I asked.

"Begob, they've nothing finer to wear in Heaven," he said, and added hastily, "Barring the blessed saints."

"I'm writing a book about Ireland," I told him.

"Then," said Old Mickey, "you've the grandest country in the whole world to write about."

"I have," I said, "but no one will read it unless I tell them one thing. It's the one thing they will want to know."

"And what's that?" asked Old Mickey.

"It's what the people themselves think about this new form of government we've got," I said.

"Begob, you're right," said Old Mickey. "It's what they'll want to know."

"And I've come to you to ask you," I said, "because I was sure you'd know."

"Sure, I know it well enough," he said. "Hist, and I'll tell you."

I stood and waited, and there was silence.

"And what is it?" I asked.

"Wait now," said Old Mickey, "wait till I get my pipe drawing well, for sometimes it does be getting choked. And wait till those young lads have gone by. They've no call to be overhearing what I say to a gentleman."

"Shall we come into your house?" I asked.

"We will not," he said. "For if we were to do that, wouldn't everyone know we'd gone in to talk politics? We'll wait here and they'll soon be gone by."

And the old man turned the tobacco out of his pipe and earnestly prodded the deeps of the bowl with the point of an old nail. And the young men went by.

"Look now. It's like this," said Old Mickey.

But something in the way he had prodded his pipe had given the impression that he was only waiting to talk politics, for one of the three young men that had strolled by turned very leisurely round again and very slowly indeed began to stray back, and listlessly the others came after him.

"Ah, no matter now," said Old Mickey. "You won't be writing your book all in one day. Won't some other time do?"

"It will indeed," I said. "The book needn't be finished much before next spring."

"Then one time's as good as another," said Old Mickey, "and I'll tell you next time you come."

"Any day will do," I said. "I'll come and see you next week."

With that we parted, I deciding to do as I'd said, unless I got the necessary information from some-one else in the meantime.

As I left Cranogue I saw leaning against a wall

a man to whom I had once sent a brace of ducks;
we recognized one another, and I stopped the car
to talk to him. And he was evidently still grateful
for the ducks and kindly wanting to pay me the
highest compliment in his power, for his whole
face lit up and he shouted out to me, "Aren't you
terrible fat!" It was, I am glad to say, an exaggeration; but there is no greater compliment than
this where the principal possessions for ages have
been cattle, which are valued by their fatness, and
he had felt I deserved the compliment on account
of the ducks.

"And what brings you to these parts?" he asked
me.

"I came to ask Old Mickey about the state of the
country," I said.

"Politics, is it?" said he.

"Yes," I replied.

"Ah, what do you want with politics," he said,
"when you've all the sport you want? Don't the
ducks be coming in well to that pond of yours?
I heard they were. And cubbing will be starting
in a few days."

"I'm afraid I'm writing a book about Ireland,"
I said.

"God save us," he answered. "Well, there's no
one better able to tell you how things are going
than Old Mickey, if it's politics you want."

"I don't," I said, "but no one will want to read

my book if I don't tell them what the people really think about the government we have since the country got a new name."

"I wouldn't be bothering with politics," he said. "Why don't you tell them instead the good things you hear people saying, the like of which you'd hear in no other country in the world."

"I might do both," I said.

And his idea struck me as a good one, for there has been a succession of wits in Ireland in my time, and, for the matter of that, probably all through history; but I need not trouble with the tales of the earlier ones, for many of them are likely to be in books already. When I was young the stories of Irish wit that went from mouth to mouth seemed mostly to originate with Father Hely, as for instance his devastating answer to a woman to whom he was introduced, who tediously said to him, "I hear you say funny things, Father Hely. Won't you say something funny to me?"

A difficult situation for any man to rise to, for wit is not often inspired by such dull remarks. But Father Hely rose to it.

"Indeed and I'm very pleased to see you, Mrs. Murphy," he said. "And isn't that funny, now?"

Of the innumerable sparks of his wit the one that shines clearest in my memory now is a remark he made to a farmer whom he met by chance one day, a man to whom he had once sold a horse.

"And how's the horse doing, that you got from me?" asked Father Hely.

"Ah, he's all right, your reverence," said the farmer, "but for a touch of vernacular."

And I have seen people contented with jokes that depended on nothing more than one word being mistaken for another; though why they should be called jokes I don't know, their favorable reception really depending on the pleasant superiority of noting that the farmer ought to have said navicular.

But Father Hely replied, "Now the only beast I heard of that ever had that complaint was Balaam's ass."

The successor to Father Hely was perhaps Dr. Mahaffy, the Provost of Trinity College. There is told a remark of his that always seems to me the most devastating remark ever made by one man to another. It was when he was Vice-provost of Trinity College, and Senior Fellow. He had heard an undergraduate swearing. It was Dr. Mahaffy's duty to reprove him, but not easy to go one better, for to begin with there is a certain intensity in such language, and the Vice-provost being a clergyman was quite debarred from competing. But he was more than equal to the occasion.

"Are you aware," he said, "that by swearing you endanger your immortal soul; and, *what is more important,* incur a fine of half a crown?"

Though I've said that Dr. Mahaffy was debarred from competing in bad language, yet it is on record that he used a bad word once. He was walking down Sackville Street, when a detachment of the Salvation Army met him: the officer came up to him and said, "Sir, you may wear a white tie, but I have to ask you: Are you saved?"

"Yes," said Mahaffy, "but it was a damned near thing, and I don't like to talk of it."

Once good stories were being told by others, in Mahaffy's presence, till there came one good story whose teller suddenly doubted if it would quite do for reverend ears; and, suddenly breaking off, he said, "But you are a clergyman, aren't you, Dr. Mahaffy?"

"A little," he said.

I think that he must have spoken truly; for once when he was preaching a sermon about the apostles and came to where St. Paul arrived in Athens and taught there, he became so incensed that men not educated in the classics should presume to attempt to convert the ancient Greeks, that he grew in his indignation quite pro-pagan, and was inhibited by his bishop from preaching any more sermons for a short period.

Once when he was staying with me he wanted to see a small church some distance away, so we motored there on Sunday for the service. The organ was wheezy, the singing in different styles,

and we certainly had a rather doleful hymn. A
chess-player could not have pulled out a board and
played a quiet game of chess during that hymn,
a journalist could not have written an article while
they were singing it, a lawn-tennis player could
not have practised a few shots down the aisle; but
Mahaffy followed his profession with perfect de-
corum, he kneeled down and buried his face in his
hands, and remained in silent prayer till the hymn
was over.

The modern successor to the Irish wits is, I
should say, Oliver Gogarty, though I should like
to see a competition for that succession between
him and Lord Castlerosse. To sit at dinner with
Oliver Gogarty is to be entertained by many personalities which he will assume in the course of the
evening. I have seen him, for instance, in a smok-
ing-room turn suddenly into a didactic Highland
laird showing a novice how a stag ought to be
stalked. The stalk was a very good one, advantage
being taken of every scrap of cover provided by
any chair that was met on the way; indeed, after
a short homily in a whisper, the laird was actually
about to shoot, when he noticed that his gillie had
neglected to bring his rifle. The oaths that then
broke out from the thwarted sportsman made one
forget that a Dublin surgeon was talking in a smok-
ing-room; they somehow seemed too breezy for
four walls.

Gogarty was an undergraduate at Trinity under
Mahaffy, and there, when Mahaffy's dog died, he
composed its funeral oration, "On the Death of
Diogenes, the Doctor's Dog," a poem which shows
his wit playing amongst the lore of the Greeks and
rudely mimicking Swinburne as it goes. One of
the verses is:

> For the dead dog no home is
>   Unless that it be
> Where the cat's hecatomb is
>   Of pork-butchery
> Where spaniels are sundered for sausage, ful-
>   filled of catastrophe.

Such verse was written under a pseudonym; indeed he had many pseudonyms, for one might have
been discovered, and, had it been known that he
wrote light verse, it would have wrecked his practise as a surgeon. But now perhaps his surgical
skill has overcome such fears, or the fact that
Gogarty writes light verse (amongst other verse)
is known in too many lands for his pseudonyms to
be any longer a camouflage, so that what I have
quoted here will not blast his reputation; and, even
if there were any danger of this, people have only
to look at him to realize that levity is far from his
nature, so that I must have been writing of somebody else of the same name. For the rest I may

refer readers to his own latest book, for I understand that a book about Ireland by Oliver Gogarty
will appear before this one of mine. He told me
that he was quoting in it a line or two of a verse of
mine, that has not hitherto been in print or any
form of writing. I said to him, "The lines are injudicious, and very nearly libelous, and far better
left out; but what is serious is that, quoting from
memory, you've got the rhythm wrong, although
the sense is all right; and I must insist that you put
that right."

For, whatever one says one can defend, but
against misquotation one is powerless.

Gogarty promised to do as I asked, and an
anxiety was lifted from my mind.

I will append an invitation of my own that I
once sent to him asking him to dine with me in
County Meath, a copy of which I found the other
day amongst light scraps in a drawer wherein such
things lie. Two allusions in it may need explanation; the reference to the street and to the port:
there was a civil war going on at the time, and
Gogarty had been forbidden port by some severer
doctor. Gogarty is, of course, a throat specialist.

> Ah, let the tonsils grow,
>   And come and dine with me;
> Even at best, you know,
>   They last as short as we.

Leave too the well-armed street
  To let its battle roar;
Turn to the fields your feet,
  Leave sore throats to be sore.

Let, let the tonsils grow,
  To have their little span
Of three score years or so
  And last as long as man.

Here in the fertile land
  The port you may not touch
Waits you, and by my hand
  The wild duck slain and such.

Ah, let the tonsils grow
  A few more hours, and then
Whip 'em out with the mot,
  Who lasts as long as men?

To write of Ireland without saying anything of
its humor would be to deal with the topic as incom-
pletely as if one told of the Bog of Allen without
any mention of heather; but I can claim no com-
pleteness for my brief list; for, apart from many
known names that I must have omitted, there are
the million, or more, of unknown Irishmen all
capable of illuminating a fact with wit, so that it
may be the more clearly seen and its meaning interpreted. That ability is perhaps the most conspicuous thing about Ireland. A treasure of all

countries is their daily events, and the everlasting laws out of which they arise. To perceive these things to the full is to live fully. But how perceive them? A thing truly witty is never said without throwing a light upon some one of man's ways, and sometimes showing the relation between his acts and his destiny. Even though exaggeration is used, and amply, the light will still be there, turned brightly on some man's act, even showing his character with the single flash. This brilliance is peculiarly the gift of the people of Ireland, and is confined to no class or calling, but is more widely spread there than the knowledge of reading or writing. And not only exaggeration may be an ingredient of this wit, but even absurdity may give it a spice; and perhaps we cannot always say of absurdity whether it is below or above common sense. Here is an example of it, that the reader may make head or tail of as best he can. An Englishman arrived at a station in Dublin, and looking, no doubt, for what must be dear to a methodical man, the time, but finding it variously interpreted, said to a porter, "Look here! What is the good of having two clocks if they are both different times?"

"And what," said the porter, "would be the good of having two clocks, if they were both the same time?"

When you come to think of it, the topic of these men's discussion was nonsense, but even that med-

ium of conversational art revealed in the Englishman an interest in the practical, and in the Irishman a more imaginative view. If I am wrong in
calling it nonsense, perhaps the reader may be able
to make some sense out of what either of them was
saying; but I can't.

And now it occurs to me that between a sense
for the practical, in which England excels, and a
sense for wit or philosophy or the long views that
the East takes, there must usually be a gulf. For
a man who is hourly occupied with important business has little leisure for the wider view that sees
so much besides the matter in hand, while the man
in the bow-window cannot easily be lured away to
peer through a crack. Perhaps the two attitudes
may best be observed in Ireland, unseparated by
the gulf, at any place where a man is selling a
horse: there you will hear those scraps of wisdom,
that in their legendary journeys the races which
settled in Ireland perhaps brought from the East,
and there you will find a close interest in pounds,
shillings and pence, not unworthy of the great mar-
kets of the City of London. And let me here make
public a method of business that may not be known
in London: when, at the end of suitable talk, the
horse is sold for £100, the seller will give back ten.
The advantage of this is obvious. You can always
say afterwards, "I sold that horse for £100." You
have even the check to show. You are in a more

solid position than a man who can only say he got ninety. And yet I do not suppose there is much about business, of which I am able to inform the City of London.

I was alluding just now to eastern philosophy, while speaking of the Irish point of view; and this touch of the East that there is in Irish thought, and which with A. E. was far more than a touch, is something not to be lost sight of when thinking of Ireland. Seamus MacCall in his book *And So Began The Irish Nation* tells of a queer current that he had himself observed off the coast of the north of Spain, which tended, he says, to carry seafarers wide of England and to bring them to land in the outermost of the British Isles. This tallies also with what legend tells us—that wanderers from the furthest end of the Mediterranean came to Ireland. They came also from the African coast, and there is still in County Cork a legend that claims for certain districts in the county that they were populated from Barbary. But, whatever history or legend says, one can see clearly enough in the minds of the Irish people a certain lore, a wise way of looking at things, which in greater or lesser degree all peasantries have, but which seems to me to come from the East and which shines now and then in their talk, like flashes from gold that has come from a far country. I once mentioned this Oriental trait in the Irish to no less an authority than Kipling, who said to me: "By every test that I know, the Irish are Oriental." I do not quote his words as historical proof, nor would he have liked them to be so quoted; but I give them as showing the view that was formed of this people by one who knew India, and indeed the whole world, so well. I cannot at this moment think of any piece of wisdom that has shone in conversations that I have had on roads and in lanes of Ireland, or along the edges of bogs; only I know that I have only to go out and ask some question of any man that I meet, to get in the answer some unexpected light on the topic that will in all probability show an aspect of it that is bright enough or true enough to be well worthy of notice. Modern ways may change this: indeed the change may be taking place quicker than I can notice it; for if a man is given his point of view every morning, and, in a little more exciting form, every evening, he may cease to form his own, or even to be able to; much reading, in fact, may rest the mind as comfortably as pre-digested food (whatever that may mean) may rest the digestion. The best education is that which is given at universities; but, when you come to look for the second best, there is a great deal to be said for illiteracy, for that compels a man to do his own thinking. It encourages him also to listen to tales told by the fireside at evening, and no such tales come far down the ages without having some

merit about them: they have to be what I shall call
timeworthy, as a far-traveling ship must be sea-
worthy, or they will soon be sunk by the years.
And speaking of tales reminds me of another
prominent feature about Ireland. It is a country
that may be called the land of unlikely events. "It
could only happen in Ireland," are words so often
heard that the phrase would seem to call for in-
vestigation; and whether the queer originality is
in Irish actions, or in the way that they tell of
them, there are certainly very queer tales to be
heard in Ireland. I will tell a little fishing-story
as an example of this, or perhaps I should call it a
dog-story. Looking into the distance from Tara
I should be able to see the place where it occurred,
if only I could identify it in that vast panorama.
There was a man with a dog who would retrieve
anything, and with neighbors to whom he told
many a story of his dog's unequaled abilities; and
maybe the neighbors bided their time, and waited
for a story of their own. And this was the story.
One day the owner of the supernatural dog went
fishing in the Boyne, with a lump of dynamite at
the end of a stick, and a Bickford fuse attached.
Having lit the fuse he threw the stick as far as he
could into the Boyne. Then the faithful dog retrieved it, and came joyfully seeking his master
with the stick in his mouth, and the fuse burning
towards a bomb large enough to kill fish. The

story dwells with some zest on the fisherman's run over a wide field to the nearest path, to find a stone to throw at the self-satisfied dog.

In this frivolous story is there not almost a Greek element, as though Nemesis had grown bored with the fisherman's tales of his dog, and had yawned at last and turned the dog against him? Is there not also a certain symmetry in the unconventionality of the man and the dog?

And here is another story from the Land of Unlikely Events: an Irish lady told me that one day a man came to see her, coming rather late in the evening, when nobody was about; he had quarreled with his priest, and so wanted to change his religion, and had come to the Big House to ask the lady what religion he had best take instead. First she had tried to see if the quarrel could not be healed; and, when she found it couldn't, she gave him the advice that he sought.

"And what religion did you choose for him?" I asked her.

"Well, I didn't like to recommend ours," she said, "because that would have been too obvious, and you know they always count on us to be fair. So I advised the Salvation Army."

"And did he take your advice?" I asked.

"Of course he did," she replied. "And he came to me some weeks later, and said that it suited him grand."

I will not give my readers any more Irish stories, unless some occur to my mind as I write; for, though they season a discourse as cloves season an apple pie, one would hesitate to open a pie that was made of cloves. But let me tell my reader one secret about Irish stories, a thing unknown to any Englishman whom I have ever met, a little secret but one profoundly hidden: and that is that the words "I will be after doing" this or that, so often met with in stories about Ireland, are impossible in the mouth of an Irishman. If you read or hear those words, then it was not an Irishman that wrote or told that tale. If you read such words in a book, and the name of a well-known Irishman is on the cover, then you may be sure that the book was written for him by somebody living in London, who next year may be writing *My Memories as a Chaplain,* and, in time for the autumn publications, *My Forty Years on the Turf.* For, "I will be after doing something" would mean "I will be having done it," which, though possibly not beyond the utmost stretch of grammar, would be far too clumsy for any conversation. This secret seems never to have been revealed before, and nearly half the Irish stories one hears in England contain this curious future-past tense.

The typical Irishman will not be met in these pages, chiefly because there is no such thing; for, although the amount greatly varies, men are made with too much individuality and idiosyncrasy for it to be possible to find one so convenient for handling as the typical man or the average man, though we often hear of him. And another reason why you will not meet the typical Irishman is that he is dead: he was the first Irishman that I can ever remember seeing on Irish soil, or rather on Irish timber, for I never remember seeing him off the platform at Kingstown, except once when I saw him in Hyde Park. He was Davy Stephens, and I think that the profession of typical Irishman was one that he deliberately chose, for he was the first Irishman that most people saw on arriving in Ireland, never being absent from Kingstown Pier with a bundle of newspapers under his arm as the boats arrived. He had aquiline features, and any wildness there may have been in his eye was admirably enhanced by the long ringlets that he wore nearly down to his shoulders. On one day in every year this wild figure assumed a splendid tidiness, and went in frock-coat and tall hat to see the Derby, spending the rest of the day on a seat in Hyde Park, whence he could watch the splendor of the gentry in their natural surroundings, instead of seeing them only by twos and threes, muffled up, cold and sleepy, as they came from the boat.

As I said, there is no such thing as the typical Irishman; but, as people are often looking for one, it may well have occurred to Davy Stephens to show them what they were looking for, and before they had penetrated any further into Ireland than the end of Kingstown Pier. Poor old Davy Stephens; how many thousands of wintry dawns he must have seen rising over the sea, and shining bright and clear on the houses of Kingstown; how many winds must have shrilled in his ringlets; and then one day there must have blown one that at last was too cold for him.

V

Francis Ledwidge

ONCE in the Sahara some Arabs were telling me the names of the stars and explaining how they had come by them, when, pointing eastwards from our little encampment, they showed me a star that had risen a short way from the horizon, and that soon, they told me, would set. I do not tell the story of that star as I heard it beside our fire, for it has no concern with this story; but I remember its bright brief light looking over the desert, and, remembering it now, I think of Ledwidge. And I remember on that same journey a flight of birds heard suddenly over the waste, where there were no trees for them for hundreds of miles; I remember their sudden voices; and they sped on northwards and there was dead silence again. Indeed all beautiful things that were swift in their coming, and brief, remind me of Ledwidge.

In the summer of 1912, I received a letter from him and a copybook full of his verse, asking my opinion of it. In that book there were immaturities, showing how young he was; trite phrases amongst unfaltering lines and piercingly keen per-

ceptions of the Irish countryside. It was as though
an eager child had brought one bundles of rare
flowers, mixed with a few weeds. There is so little
advice that one can give to a young poet (for one
cannot make a poet with advice) that probably all
the advice I ever gave him was to leave out these
trite phrases, which he immediately did. Looking
again at the small collection of verse that he has
left on this side of Lethe, I see at least one of these
phrases among the earlier poems. But he never
used them through any weakness of the power to
make phrases of his own, or any shortness of vision;
but merely because they happened to be there,
amongst some bad reading that he had probably
done, like the weeds that I have mentioned among
the flowers. It was every bit as easy for him to
invent a beautiful metaphor such as,

> The large moon rose up queenly as a flower
>   Charmed by some Indian pipes,

as it was to use the expression "bow before the
blast"; and, when I suggested to him choosing in
preference such things as the former, he made that
choice and abided by it. The brilliance of the
vision that he had of the fields he knew immediately astonished me. I remember still my surprise
at reading:

> When briars make semicircles on the way.

Like most people I had known briars all my life, and knew the curves that their tendrils made on a path; and yet I had never seen it written that they made semicircles, or heard it said, though when I read that line I immediately realized that they did; that is to say I realized that an eye keener than mine had looked at them. And this was an experience that I was to have repeatedly when reading Ledwidge's poetry. Of all those early lines the ones that thrilled me most were:

> And wondrous impudently sweet,
> Half of him passion, half conceit,
> The blackbird calls adown the street.

I have not seen any merrier, truer description of a blackbird, in all I have ever read. One might well say of all his verse what he says of the poet in spring:

> And in his song you hear the river's rhyme
> And the first bleat of the lamb.

I wrote to him greeting him as a true poet, and he was intensely grateful for this, and never forgot that gratitude, though a lark owes nothing to us for knowing that he is a lark. How he looked at nature, his deep feeling for it and his ability to preserve for us something of it in books, may be suggested by a verse of one of those earlier poems called, "To a Linnet in a Cage."

When Spring is in the fields that stained your wing,
  And the blue distance is alive with song,
And finny quiets of the babbling spring
  Rock lilies red and long,
At dewy daybreak, I will set you free
  In ferny turnings of the woodbine lane,
Where faint-voiced echoes leave and cross in glee
  The hilly swollen plain.

In the next verse come the lovely lines

You want the wide air of the moody noon
And the slanting evening showers.

Indeed his verse is full of lovely lines, and anyone with much love of rural things might find on
page after page of his book single lines that if collected would keep alive the memory of bright
meadows starred with flowers, quite as vividly as
the flowers themselves could do it when pressed
between pages, as some preserve them for a memory of past seasons. And here is another line taken
from one of those first poems, that tells of the
coming of Spring:

The golden news the skylark waketh

I was in London when I received the letter of
which I spoke, but shortly afterwards I returned
to Ireland and first saw Ledwidge. He came over
from Slane, whose wooded hill standing above the

Boyne is one of the hills that one can see from Tara,
lying between the Mourne Mountains and the hills
of northwest Meath, going pale blue into Cavan;
but much nearer than either. He belonged definitely to one of the Irish types, having the features
of one of the races that populate Ireland; but,
though they are familiar to me, I do not know
which race it is. One thing, however, set him
apart from other men that one meets, and that was
his eyes. Poets usually have fine eyes, but I never
saw eyes with pupils in which there was more
room for dreams.

I gave him a copy of Keats' poems, and almost
at once I thought that I detected an improvement
in his poems, a kind of echo such as stirs faintly in
bells when another is ringing beside it; no more
than that, for he imitated nobody; but I think that
his spirit was strengthened by meeting the spirit of
Keats. It would be a fitting description to call him
wayward: he seems to have sought occupations as
a butterfly seeks flowers; and wayward he continued. I never found anybody more full of gratitude for the little things one could do for them, a
gratitude that did not arise from any benevolence
in me, but from the intense friendliness of his own
spirit; and no one can read his verses without finding that bubbling over from them. In life he had
a most intense devotion to his mother, and in his
art his greatest love seemed to be for the song of

the blackbird. I made a collection of his poems and took them to the firm of publishers who sponsor them to this day, Messrs. Herbert Jenkins.

The manager in those days was Mr. Jenkins. He made an error which I wish to correct now. He advertised Francis Ledwidge very widely as "the scavenger poet." One does not like to correct the errors of men who are dead; but Ledwidge is also dead, and I owe it to his memory to say that he was never a scavenger. He was employed at the time on work on the roads under the County Council in Meath; but workmen on roads are not scavengers, moreover Francis Ledwidge was foreman of the gang. The firm of Messrs. Herbert Jenkins, as at present constituted, have never suggested that Ledwidge was a scavenger or issued any other mistaken description of him.

Here is one of the early poems that appeared in that first book:

DESIRE IN SPRING

I love the cradle songs the mothers sing
In lonely places when the twilight drops,
The slow endearing melodies that bring
Sleep to the weeping lids; and, when she stops,
I love the roadside birds upon the tops
Of dusty hedges in a world of Spring.

And when the sunny rain drips from the edge
Of midday wind, and meadows lean one way,

And a long whisper passes through the sedge,
Beside the broken water let me stay,
While these old airs upon my memory play,
And silent changes color up the hedge.

He had an intense simplicity. But let us not
think ourselves too grand for him on that account.
We have all seen a wind blowing over deep meadows, but which of us has ever recorded a fact more
vividly than he has with those simple words "and
meadows lean one way"? But there was another
thing that he knew besides the grass and the trees
and the flowers and birds and sheep; he knew the
mind of the people, of whom he was one, and was
as familiar with the fancies that lived therein as he
was with the robins and linnets. One sees again
and again throughout these poems hints of a knowledge of two things very near to the hearts of the
Irish people; old legend, to which they are always
leaning back, and the haunting presence of fairies
and all manner of spirits, of which they speak
rarely to me, but which must have been as well
known to Ledwidge as the birds that sing by the
Boyne. I do not know how the Lanaun Shee are
faring now; they may have been poisoned by politics, or the ether may be too full of jazz from
Droitwich and Athlone for them to move as easily
as they used, without continually jostling their
elbows against reality; but when Ledwidge wrote

they evidently came at times very near to the folk amongst whom he lived, none of whom would have been likely to find anything particularly odd in the statement that

> Every night at Currabwee
> Little men with leather hats
> Mend the boots of faery.

And any one interested in that form of cobbling may be glad to hear that

> Louder than a cricket's wing
> All night long their hammers' glee
> Times the merry songs they sing.

Certainly the flashes that shine out here and there in Ledwidge's poems are from a golden hoard of folk-lore; but little of it will be found in this book of mine, for I have only seen glimpses and hints of it, while to Ledwidge it was a treasure that he shared with probably all his neighbors. That first book was a little bunch of idylls inspired almost only by two things, the rural beauty of the fields that lie about the Boyne, where it flows east again after its journey northward, whose journey Tara watches all the way; and by the heroic legends of those who lived once on Tara. Almost only by these that book is inspired, though now and then some influence from old books he had read would stray for a moment amongst his rustic lines;

and one poem I think now that I should not have
included in the collection, as it is unmistakably influenced by Mr. Walter de la Mare's poem "The
Listeners," a poem that could hardly fail to influence a very young poet.

A very short while passed, and things went badly
with the world, and Ledwidge's art was greatly
strengthening.   Ledwidge took part in the patriotic
fervor that soon filled Kitchener's first army, but
before he enlistened in an Irish regiment, the Royal
Inniskilling Fusiliers, he had been reading Keats,
from whom he had probably learned the name of
Artemis and other goddesses, and he wrote a poem
called "The Dream of Artemis"; but, for all the
classical allusions in that poem, his inspiration was
still from the fields of Meath, a rose that could
never be transplanted to climb the pillars of any
Greek temple, yet enriched by winds from Olym-
pus.   This poem is such a lovely description of a
hunt followed by a young man and a goddess that
I will quote a great deal of it:

The white Nine left the spaces of flowers, and now
Went calling through the wood the hunter's call.
Young echoes sleeping in the hollow bough
Took up the shouts and handed them to all
Their sisters of the crags, 'til all the day
Was filled with voices loud and musical.
I followed them across a tangled way
'Til the red deer broke out and took the brow

Of a wide hill in bounces like a ball.
Beside swift Artemis I joined the chase;
We roused up kine and scattered fleecy flocks;
Crossed at a mill a swift and bubbly race;
Scaled in a wood of pine the knotty rocks;
Past a gray vision of a valley town;
Past swains at labor in their colored frocks;
Once saw a boar upon a windy down;
Once heard a cradle in a lonely place,
And saw the red flash of a frightened fox.

We passed a garden where three maids in blue
Were talking of a queen a long time dead.
We caught a green glimpse of the sea: then through
A town all hills; now round a wood we sped
And killed our quarry in his native lair.
Then Artemis spun round to me and said,
"Whence come you?" and I took her long damp hair
And made a ball of it, and said, "Where you
Are midnight's dreams of love."

Then follow lines telling of the love of this mortal
for the immortal; love in the evening, when

> The trees were all at peace,
> And lifting slowly on the gray evetide
> A large and lovely star.

And there comes a lovely little bit of autobiography
in the lines:

I have not loved on Earth the strife for gold,
Nor the great name that makes immortal man,

But all that struggle upward to behold
What still is left of Beauty undisgraced,
The snowdrop at the heel of winter cold
And shivering, and the wayward cuckoo chased
By lingering March, and, in the thunder's van
The poor lambs merry on the meager wold,
By-ways and cast-off things that lie therein,
Old boots that trod the highways of the world,
The schoolboy's broken hoop, the battered bin
That heard the ragman's story, blackened places
Where gipsies camped and circuses made din,
Fast water and the melancholy traces
Of sea tides.

So far is he from borrowing inspiration from others
and trying to write about Greece that, knowing
Meath as I do and knowing where he lived, I can
almost follow the hunt. That intensely vivid description of a deer going over the hill "in bounces
like a ball" would be in Slane deer-park, then they
would have crossed the Boyne; and even people
"talking of a queen a long time dead" are not at
all foreign to Ireland where, as I think I have said
already, memories are continually turning backwards to legends as far and as dim as the Slieve
Blooms seen from Tara. That poem suddenly
ends with the two surprising lines:

Oh, Artemis—what grief the silence brings!
I hear the rolling chariot of Mars!

Then he enlisted and came to Richmond Bar-
racks, to the 5th battalion of the Inniskillings.   A
simple fancy that came to him at this time, a soldier
about to go to the war, is so quaint and beautiful
that I will quote the whole of it. It is called "To
a Little Boy in the Morning." I do not know who
the boy was, perhaps a little brother who had died.

He will not come, and still I wait.
He whistles at another gate
Where angels listen. Ah, I know
He will not come, yet if I go
How shall I know he did not pass
Barefooted in the flowery grass?

The moon leans on one silver horn
Above the silhouettes of morn,
And from their nest sills finches whistle
Or stooping pluck the downy thistle.
How is the morn so gay and fair
Without his whistling in its air?

The world is calling, I must go.
How shall I know he did not pass
Barefooted in the shining grass?

He fought in Gallipoli and Greece and France,
still writing poems and still taking with him a
vivid memory of his home, that seemed almost un-
troubled by the war. He tells of the sheep coming
home in Greece, jumping "With one bell-ring o'er

the brooks." That is an example of his art, a very
simple thing put simply and very clearly, and yet
a thing that no one seems to have thought of saying
before. It is unquestionably true; for, when you
come to think of it, the sheep's jump would shove
the bell back against his neck, and it would ring
no more till he landed on the other side. Ledwidge, of course, never thought of it, he merely
had the impression, and that impression remained
so clear on his sensitive spirit that we get it recorded exactly as this simple event occurred. This
is a poem that he wrote in France, nearly his last,
which shows how completely he cloaked himself
with the Irish atmosphere and carried it always
with him.

HOME

A burst of sudden wings at dawn,
Faint voices in a dreamy noon,
Evenings of mist and murmurings,
And nights with rainbows of the moon.
And through these things a wood-way dim,
And waters dim, and slow sheep seen
On uphill paths that wind away
Through summer sounds and harvest green.

This is a song a robin sang
This morning on a broken tree,
It was about the little fields
That call across the world to me.

Only one word in the poem shows that it was written on a battlefield during the Great War. The robin sang on a broken tree, and but for that one word "broken" the poem would be an idyll of peace. His last poem began with the words

> Powdered and perfumed the full bee
> Winged heavily across the clover,
> And where the hills were dim with dew,
> Purple and blue the west leaned over.

I quote the lines in order to show to what strength his art had come. The poem told how the girl that he loved and who had died in the summer of 1915 appeared to him, and that he knew then that his life must be at an end. He says:

> I tiptoed gently up and stooped
> Above her looped and shining tresses,
> And asked her of her kin and name,
> And why she came from fairy places.
> She told me of a sunny coast
> Beyond the most adventurous sailor,

And the verses tell of a land strange and lovely but not too strange to be easily seen by an Irish imagination. One verse tells of that country thus:

> Nor Autumn with her brown line marks
> The time of larks, the length of roses,
> But song-time there is over never
> Nor flower-time ever, ever closes.

And these lovely lines are there:

> And by the lakes the skies are white,
>   (Oh, the delight!) when swans are coming.

I turn to the last page of his book, and find him still looking at nature with a poet's eye.

> Like a poor widow whose late grief
> Seeks for relief in lonely byways,
> The moon, companionless and dim,
> Took her dull rim through starless highways.

And low on that last page still speaking of the girl whose spirit had come for him, he writes:

> From hill to hill, from land to land,
> Her lovely hand is beckoning for me,
> I follow on through dangerous zones,
> 'Cross dead men's bones and oceans stormy.

The reader will recognize for himself, and I think delight in, the inferior rhyme in those lines like echoes ringing on deep in a bell after the bell has spoken.

It is no use lamenting what is irretrievably lost, yet the thought is often with me that the small harvest of those early years and the easy fluency with which he wrote and the increasing number of beautiful lines to the page, as those few years went by, show that here were the makings of a great poet, whom the world will not know now. It may

be that he will come to a great reputation yet, as
though a prophecy of his own were fulfilled:

> At dawn a bird will waken me
> Unto my place among the kings.

VI

How the Students Came to Trim

I HAVE written a good deal about poets, because I feel that it is not in old buildings, slowly being destroyed by ivy, in which Ireland's character lies; nor even only in its hills and valleys; for scenery has an intensity when shining out of a poet's spirit, and even an immortality there, that is equal to its material one. I look, in fact, as much for Ireland in the Irish mind as I do in the Irish fields. Much may pass over a field and leave no trace, but what wonderful tracks we may see where a fancy has passed over a mind, if only we can discover it. A people are often very secret, but we must try to find their secrets if we venture to write a book about them. Poets fortunately share their secrets with us: in Ledwidge we find the Irish fields shining, in A. E. we see the Irish races looking back over their shoulders eastwards, and in James Stephens we find qualities not amiss in those spirits that dance over Irish bogs, whom Puck would cheerfully recognize as his equals. Yet to tell of Ireland one must tell of Ireland in stone as well as Ireland in dream; though it is right to put poetry first, for that is the dream in the raw, while towers

62

and spires are but the casts of dreams preserved in material things, as long as material things are able to last.

Standing on Tara there is ample choice of ancient buildings within the huge circle of the view; not that many buildings can be picked out with the eye, except the old tower of Skyrne, quite close, to the east, and the church of St. Patrick upon the hill itself, and a tower on the horizon to the north-west, and the white spire of Trim cathedral, very visible when once discovered; all else is grass and woods, watched over far away by the ghosts of mountains. We will go to Trim, where the white spire shows the way. As we go westwards all the land dips with us. Looking west from Tara there lie familiar fields to the left, green fields and clumps of trees, with a yellowish-green field, here and there, that has haycocks in it and is brighter than all the others, as though it had attracted the sun; fields near and neighborly, tended by man, fields without mystery.

And suddenly the land plunges to distance. At the very edge of a common field quite close, the remote West frowns, mountains appear and dis-appear with varying moods of the evening, and immediately beyond the fields that are so clear and known appear fields touched with a silvery-greeny color, that seem almost to suggest the feet of the fairies as more to be expected than the plow. Down this sudden dip we go on our way westwards, and the land grows wilder as we go. We are going along the edge of the Pale, the land that the Normans tidied, and held with a ring of castles, in one of which I live; and at the westernmost point of it they built their strongest fortress, the castle of Trim, as though they feared what lay to the west and massed their greatest strength against it. Through land fast becoming wilder we approach Trim; the bogs are nearer and the rushy fields; but I have chosen that road because it is splendid with the remains of magnificent building. Between Bective and Trim one may see architecture defying Time, every mile or so, and only losing slowly.

At Bective we came to the fine bridge over the river, built with the skill that gives masonry strength to withstand time, the product of which skill is always beautiful. And that is one of the pieces of luck that we have who live in this world; that good work makes beautiful things, and good work lasts. Were it the other way about, it could only be a matter of time when the world would grow too hideous for anybody to live in. On the right bank of the river, and on the left-hand side of the road, a little row of cottages runs down to the edge of the water, and on the other side stands Bective Abbey. The walls of the ruined abbey hold out stoutly still against time, but the little cottages seem to have tired of the struggle and have

RUINS OF BECTIVE ABBEY, NEAR TRIM, COUNTY MEATH

GATHERING PEAT FOR FUEL IN A VALLEY NEAR MACROOM

mostly gone the way of so much else that hears the southwest wind sighing softly over our fields. So men have left them and weeds have come in instead, except to one which has the appearance of being shared by both. In another of them the weeds are completely triumphant, but I do not think that the owner felt he was beaten by them, for he inscribed in white paint on his lintel "Up Sinn Fein." And the inscription survives, though roof and door are down.

As one goes across the river to Bective Abbey one needs no knowledge of history to see that the holy men for whom it was built had fear of grosser things than spiritual dangers, for though they prayed in their chapels they had battlements on their towers, and walls of great thickness. They obviously feared some mundane danger. If Ireland was entirely a land of saints twenty-five years or so before the Normans came, then the Cistercians misjudged them, for they housed themselves in a fortress. Nor are the battlements and towers merely symbolical, or built for ornament, but obviously for defense. Bright green weeds grow now in its cloisters, and all the roofs are gone, but it will take many more centuries to lower the towers. Among its vaults and arches and great fireplaces one needs either knowledge of ancient history or imagination to picture how it looked once; I have no accurate knowledge of its history, and the last

time I went into it I was on my way home from a
hard day's snipe-shooting, and I was probably
tired, and my imagination was certainly asleep.

But only today I heard this piece of news: if
news be the word for it, news which, compared
with anything we can write, is what raw gold is to
the gold that jewelers use. This piece of truth that
had come down the ages as nuggets are rolled in
streams was as follows: when Henry VIII closed
the monastery at Bective, the students left it and
came to Trim, taking up half a mile of the road.
This was told me on the very road by which the
students had come; many of them were Belgian and
French, and I was told other things about them,
but it is the detail about the length of road they
took up that gleams in my memory. I doubt if the
distance is even exaggerated: I doubt if historians
get as much truth from their documents. It somehow sounds to me as something that an eye-witness
had seen and told his children, who passed it on to
their grandchildren, who passed it on again, so that
it came, with not very many old people telling the
story, to the old woman I knew, who died about
ten years ago well on in her nineties and had told
it to the man who told it to me. I do not very often
hear these stories, but they are the histories of the
cottage fireside, and are neither harmed by mold
nor bookworm nor fire, nor by anything but the
spread of the knowledge of reading and writing,

which gains ground fast in Ireland; and I fear there is coming a time when the people will know more of the praise of meat-extracts than of the pageantry of events that have brightened the ages.

At stately intervals houses stand along the Boyne, every mile or so, now as in the time of the Normans. When Bective Abbey was occupied by Cistercian monks, the castle of Assey stood a mile below it on the opposite side of the river, and the castle of Scurlockstown about two miles further up. One passes the ruins of a little church at Scurlockstown, on the right, and the ruins of a large mill on the left; one comes to a bend in the road where the Boyne sweeps by very close, with an abandoned lime-kiln on the far side of the river. Then churches and abbeys are thicker along the banks as you go up the Boyne; the monastery of Newtown upon the right bank was less than a mile from Scurlockstown, and across the river, little more than a hundred yards from the monastery, stand the ruins of what must have been a large church, with its graveyard beside it, in which people bury yet; and a quarter of a mile more brings you to the great castle of Trim, called the key of the Pale, in which King John lived when he governed Ireland for his brother Richard I. Although he was not yet King, the castle is often spoken of to this day as King John's Castle; though of recent years there have been some who, preferring the authority of

churches to that of the Crown, and feeling themselves fully justified in adapting history to useful
ends, have called it Saint John's Castle. Near by
(oh, printer, by whatever seems to you sacred I
appeal to you not to print Near By as one word)
stands the sheer front of St. Mary's church, called
the Yellow Steeple.

If an irruption breaks out on Stromboli, or war
comes to Flanders, these things must make a great
stir among the people who live there, and probably very few of them ever expected what came;
yet a history of a country, when you can sit and
read it calmly, turning over centuries easily with
your thumb, seems not to vary greatly. We are
inclined to pity the simplicity of fishermen for
building their little white houses upon the feet of
Stromboli, and yet we ourselves are surprised when
arson breaks out in Ireland. But glancing today
at a book that told of Trim, eight miles from where
I live, I came on a little brief diary of St. Mary's
Abbey, whose yellow steeple is so great a landmark,
with its one great window far up in the sky. And
there I read: 1108. In this year Connor O'Mag-
laghlin burnt the town of Trim, and above two
hundred persons, then in the church, perished in
the flames.

1127. Connor, the son of Feargul O'Lochluin,
burned the church and steeple of this abbey, both
of which were filled with unfortunate people.

1143. Trim was consumed by fire, as well as Dunshaughlin and Kildare.

And in 1155 they burned the town and the abbey again.

In 1203 Trim was again destroyed by fire.

They then seem to have had one of those splendid periods, such as we sometimes do have in Ireland, of 165 years in which nobody in Trim burned anything. And then one reads: 1368. The church of St. Mary in Trim was burnt.

In 1376 the Abbot of the church of St. Mary sued three men for burning the mill at Rathnally, the property of the said Abbot.

But, as the same book records that in 1506 the town was burned by lightning, it may well be argued that it is on account of something especially inflammable in Irish houses that they got burnt, and not on account of any taste for arson inherent in the people.

One goes for some way under the walls of King John's Castle as one comes into Trim; and where one enters it through a gateway high in the wall, to which a path is now built up, the walls rise sheer from little kitchen-gardens.

There is no hospitable look about the tower that guards the gateway; for, even in its old age, with weeds on its head and draped with a cloak of ivy, it shows clear enough the grooves through which the portcullis descended; and if one climbs to the

top, where the long slit in the limestone shows the
breadth of the portcullis, one sees behind it the
hole through which molten lead was poured down,
or whatever they used as a hint to men below to
come no further, if they had passed the portcullis.
Looking down from here on to the little gardens
one sees fine walls separating garden from garden,
for there has been abundant stone for building in
Trim, ever since the outer walls of the castle began
to crumble. Gardens looked down on from a
height seem always to me to have something in
them suggesting or hinting that they have borrowed
a ray of their brightness from some distant lovelier
world. The walls from which one looks down on
the gardens are hollow, and wide enough for troops
to move along them, with towers every fifty yards
or so, bulging out from the walls, and arrow-slits
in the towers, no mere ornamental arrow-slits, but
convenient apertures for a six-foot bow, and peering in every direction, not only to watch for men
attacking the tower they guard, but flanking any
attack on a neighboring tower; spiral staircases run
up the tower, up and up till they or the tower
crumble; and the ivy claws and struggles in its
age-long fight with the stone, and the slow drip that
makes stalactites falls in the silence of vaults. The
castle is about a third of a mile round. Going
along the walls right-handed from the tower of the
principal gateway one passes four more towers,

before one comes to the tower that faces east, guarding another gateway. And the great arrow-slits stand straight and clearly cut, where much else has crumbled, as though they were watching still, however forgetful the battlements might be; as though they were peering yet to strike at the flank of attackers. Where the wall is much crumbled an elder leans out through a gap, with such an attitude in its clutching branches as though the tree had learned to ape the customs of men and was imitating some archer looking down from the walls.

The tower that faces east has a groove for another great portcullis, and two holes for molten lead, this time in front of the portcullis; then comes a ditch that was once a moat, and a sheer drop in the tower goes where the drawbridge must once have been, and the tower with all its defenses juts out beyond the moat. This tower is full of spiral stairs and passages, and could have been a very busy place whenever disturbed by attack. The stones there are very green now, some tiny moss having clad them as brilliantly as they can have been ever adorned. In the wall between this and the next tower, at a corner of the castle which is upon the bank of the river, there used to be the Irish mint, rediscovered in 1912 when I was having such repairs done on the castle, of which I am the present owner, as would prevent the ivy actually winning its siege during this century. Along the Boyne from the tower at the northeastern corner, for at least a hundred yards, the walls are very low, for whoever was tempted to take the great stones away must have found the temptation strongest where they could be floated away in boats.

Probably most of Trim is built from this part of the wall. And then the towers begin again, looking over the Boyne. And not even ruins, nor weeds triumphing over them, nor birds taking men's place in their galleries, seem to have the power that any river has to call to the mind the passing of ages: not only the swifter the river but the more beautiful that it is, the more it seems to be sweeping the years away. The Boyne under those crumbled walls seems in certain moments just about to change from a full and shining river to the visible passage of time. In the midst of these walls and towers rises the keep, like a cluster of towers, going up so high that the voices of jackdaws disturbed from their homes sound faint to the people below. Here, amongst other rooms, with mighty walls but roofless, stands the banqueting hall, or so historians tell us, with its great fireplace blackened still. It is built of limestone; but for archways, and pillars of doors, for little shrines in the walls and niches of holy water, they used the soft red sandstone that was more easily worked. Calm, and assured of their ownership, the jackdaws float in and out of their high homes. The strength of the walls and great height, and the huge sockets for bolts running into the walls for yards, show that the keep was planned for a grim defense.

And many a defense it maintained, while under its protection there grew up the town of Trim, and a certain culture became possible which, but for that row of towers, could not have survived. There is no portcullis now in either gateway and nothing remains of the strength that protected Trim but the walls, bare but for the weeds, and the wandering spirals of stone that surmount the towers; yet they did not stand in vain, for by brute force the great castles, and by subtler means the monasteries, imposed some fear of some law, and built up more of whatever culture we have than we are perhaps ready to credit them with having achieved for us. And however convenient it be for the purpose of political speeches to divide all who are in Ireland today into the descendants of brutal Normans or savage Irish, the fact remains that we all share in as much of that culture as we have been lucky enough to retain, just as we are all descended from conqueror and conquered.

VII

A Lapse of Memory

BUT I have left too long the serious purpose of this book, which is to tell the curious reader what I believe he will most want to learn from these pages, what the Irish people really think of our new political system. I had not intended to go over to see Old Mickey again for another week or so, as he lives a bit out of my way; and, if I could get the information I required, and that the reader will require, from anyone else in the meantime, it would save me a long journey. Only, considering the importance of the topic, as it appears to me, and will certainly appear to everyone desiring information about Ireland, I had to make sure that the person to whom I went for this information would be an authority on it. Casting round my mind as to whom to consult, I suddenly thought of a neighbor, who for various reasons that I will not give, so as not to identify him too closely, was so much in touch with the people, that he would be certain to know just how they felt about this important matter. So to him I went at once, and found him looking gravely at his garden wall, wondering whether he ought to do something about it now to prevent its falling down, or whether it wouldn't last for another generation.

"Hullo," he said. "What brings you over here?"

"To tell you the truth," I said, "I wanted to know what the people really think about this new government we have. And I knew you'd know. And I know you won't mind telling me."

"What they think about it?" he said. "You aren't writing a book about it, or anything? Are you?"

"Well, I rather am," I said.

"Good God!" said he. "Well, look here; I don't mind telling you what they think about it. But you mustn't put it into your damned book. Because whenever anybody writes a book there's always some other fellow who knows just what he's at, and can trace where he's been and who he's been talking to. You see what I mean. I couldn't do it myself, but there'll be somebody who'll be able to work it all out, and he'll know it's me you've been talking to."

"I'd be as careful as I could," I said; "but I suppose it's possible."

"I'm damned sure it is," said he. "I'll tell you what I believe they think about it; in fact I've heard it from more than one of them. Only you mustn't put it in your book."

"Very well, I won't," I said; "not as coming from you. But, if I hear the same from anybody else, I'm not bound not to put in what they tell me, even if it's the same as yours, as it probably will be. And in any case Old Mickey over at Cranogue has promised to tell me, if I don't hear it from some-one else sooner."

"Old Mickey would know," said my neighbor thoughtfully.

"Yes," I said. "So, you see, there it is. I shall hear about it from him in any case, and I'm going to write what he tells me. But you may as well tell me first, and I won't quote a word from you."

I had my own idea about it all, and I was rather inquisitive to see if it was the right one.

"Well, you see," he said, "it's like this. . . ."

And he told me all about it. But I do not tell the reader in this chapter what it is, because of my promise.

"It's rather what I thought," I said. "I am going over to see Charlie in a couple of days. Do you think I'd get it from him? It would save me the trouble of going all the way to Cranogue."

"Charlie is just the fellow that would know," he answered.

So I decided to get for my reader the necessary information from that rather more distant neigh-bor whom we all call Charlie. I knew he would tell me and would not mind what I did with the information. He is one of those fellows who are always saying just what comes into their heads. I

have told him that he'll get himself shot some day;
and he doesn't seem to care.

"Thanks," I said. "I won't say a word of what
you told me, as coming from you. I'll get it all
from Charlie. And perhaps I'd better check it,
after all, with Old Mickey. One can't be too careful of one's accuracy in a matter like that."

"Well, it's just as I told you," he said.

"I know," I said, and we parted.

The more I thought of it the clearer I saw that
the opinion of the people themselves on the politics
that they have got would be the essential part of
this book. And, that decided, the sooner I got to
it the better. So, instead of waiting till the time
that he was expecting me, I determined to go over
to see Charlie as soon as I could. I sent him a
telegram suggesting tea that afternoon, and he
wired back asking me to come to lunch next day.
And when the next day came I slipped a notebook
into my pocket so as to be sure of getting his exact
words on a subject of so much importance to any
of my readers who care about Ireland at all. We
were to be alone at lunch; and unfortunately, he
told me, he had to go out soon afterwards, as he
was on a committee for investigating the conditions
in factories in that part of Meath, and the committee was meeting at three o'clock.

"A damned awkward time," he said, "but I must

go, because it was rather kind of them to put me on the committee at all, being what I am."

"But are there any factories round here?" I asked.

"Not yet," he said, "but there will be as soon as the Shannon scheme gets properly going in these parts, and we want to have the committee in running order, so as to be all ready when the factories get started. Come into the dining-room and we'll begin."

I should explain that the Shannon scheme is the building of an electric plant on the Shannon, at the cost of 6 or 7 millions, in order to provide power for the great factories of Ireland.

When I saw that my time was to be limited, I got to the business for which I had come as soon as possible; and, after inquiring about the health of his family and how his coverts were holding, I told him what I had come about.

"I was wondering," I said, "what the people themselves really think of the political situation over here."

"Yes, I wonder," he said.

"I thought you'd be the very person to know," I replied.

"Well, yes," he said, "I'm rather in touch with a few of them, so I think perhaps I do. I don't mind telling you, if you really want to know."

"Well, I rather did," I said.

"Well," he said, "I'll tell you."

When he said no more, I suppose he saw me looking at him inquiringly instead of getting on with my lunch, so he said, "Not now," with the beginnings of a look over his shoulder to where a butler and two footmen were standing. "We'll have plenty of time before I have to go."

But there was not plenty of time. Curiosity is known in all countries; and I have noticed that nothing seems to inflame it quicker than talk about politics. I can't think why, for it is a dull topic; but there it is. Those men lingered and lingered and lingered in the room, all three of them. I couldn't tell other people's servants to go, and I didn't even like to ask Charlie to, and yet as the time dragged by I realized that they were depriving me of everything I had come for, the culminating point of my whole book.

Of course I loitered about the outskirts of the subject, continually making references to it; but I could not draw him while his servants were in the room, and it did not seem to occur to him to tell them to go. To one of my remarks he said: "Why do you want to know?"

"Well, for various reasons," I said. I hardly like as a rule to say I am writing a book, because most of my friends regard a book as so silly, but he got it out of me.

"Which particular reason?" he asked.

"Well, as a matter of fact," I said, "I am writing a book about Ireland."

"Why don't you write a book about England?" he said. "It's the greatest country in the world."

"Well, the Irish say *they* are," I said.

"Every people says its own country is the greatest, I expect," he answered. "But one can prove it of England."

"What is the proof?" I asked.

"They do such damned silly things," he said, "and yet they survive. Their politicians do things that would ruin any other country; but it simply has no effect on them. They must be the greatest people in the world. No other people could stand it."

"What kind of things?" I asked.

"Oh, *all* kinds of things," he replied. "Take the Great War for instance. They all knew it was coming. They weren't so damned silly as not to know that. And how did they prepare for it?"

"How did they?" I asked.

"By disbanding as many battalions of their picked troops as possible and several batteries of artillery."

"What battalions?" I asked.

"One battalion of the Grenadiers," he said, "and another battalion of Scots Guards. And they would have disbanded the 3rd Coldstream, only that it was in Khartoum, and they didn't know

SUNSET OVER THE RIVER SHANNON AT ATHLONE

L. J. Heffernan   from Gendreau, New York

EARLY MORNING IN LIMERICK

where to find it. But if somebody hadn't hidden it, the politicians would have disbanded that too. And then look at the way they drove the North to rebellion; and went on at it till they'd made sure of civil war. That was a pretty way to be playing the fool in July, 1914, with the Kiel canal all nicely finished, and everything ready for Armageddon. They are the greatest people in the world. Nobody else could do it."

"That's a queer way of proving it," I suggested.

"Queer? Not a bit," he said. "Why queer? If you tell me a man's the greatest chess-player in the world and you show him winning a game, that doesn't prove anything. But let me see him dropping his knights on the floor and one or two of his rooks and a lot of his pawns, and perhaps a little bit drunk besides, and going on with the game and winning it in the end. Well, then I say, some player."

"Yes, I see," I said.

"It stands to reason," said Charlie. "It's the only real test. And then look at the Treaty. They threw away twenty-six counties, and didn't even trouble to see that the other side kept the treaty, as they called it."

"Why didn't they do that?" I asked.

"I'll tell you why," he said. "It's my impression that they've forgotten that they ever made a treaty."

"No, no," I said; "that's impossible. They must

know that they came to *some* arrangement about Ireland."

"I don't think so," he said. "Not the South of Ireland."

"But how could they possibly not?" I protested.

"I think they've forgotten the South of Ireland," he said.

VIII

Jack-snipe

I WAS depressed by not getting from my friend the information I wanted; for I did not get it. When eventually the servants left the dining-room we were talking of other things; and by the time I was able to break off the topic and was about to ask again for the information I came for, Charlie suddenly said: "I hope you will excuse me, but I must be off."

And sure enough it was twenty to three, and he had some way to go. There seemed nothing to do now but to make the journey to Cranogue and see Old Mickey again, and get the whole situation from him; for I could think of no one else besides him, and the two neighbors I had already consulted, whose opinion I would trust for what is the crucial point of a book that aims at giving trustworthy information upon this very thing. The mere gossip of people who were not certain to know was not a sufficient basis on which to build the information that would be expected from me on such a subject, if I were to justify my pretensions in writing this book at all. On the other hand the journey to Cranogue and back would waste the

best part of the day, and the shooting season was
well started now, and the days were getting shorter;
so that I decided to go after snipe and duck instead,
and perhaps to jot down some notes about the wild-
fowler's sport, and let the serious purpose of this
book stand over until some day when it might be
more convenient to go to Cranogue; for sport, after
all, is as much a part of Ireland as politics. So
next day I started off in the car after breakfast,
with my gamekeeper and his Labrador retriever,
and we motored to a bog a few miles away, a long
line of marsh in a fold of the land that lay between
two green slopes too small to be called hills. Years
ago when I was selling an outlying property under
the Wyndham Act, I told my tenants who had
come to see me about it that I should like to keep
the shooting rights. Their spokesman told me that
I could do that if I liked; though it was plain to
me that they were all against it. On the other hand
he pointed out to me that the advantage of giving
up the shooting rights would be that if ever I
wanted to shoot over their land I would be welcome.

Young though I was at that time I realized that
to accept those men's hospitality, which in Ireland
is boundless, would be better than to exercise any
legal right, for which nobody in Ireland ever gives
a damn. But it was not only these men's hospitality that I have enjoyed, in pursuit of sport for

many years, for it somehow spread to others, for no other reason than that hospitality of this kind is an abundant virtue of the Irish people. And so, one way and another, I have enough shooting for the whole winter. And this is varied with an occasional day's fox-hunting; days that grow fewer as my weight increases. I stopped at the farmhouse, which was on the main road; and its ancient thatch was good to see. It was perhaps a little in need of repair, for the brown straw sloped to one very deep crevasse, which was all dark black, and green with moss at the edges. And house-leeks were growing on it, which the country people say are sent for a sign that the house will never be burned; and it must be a true saying, for the juicy appearance of the fat stalk of the house-leek is an indication that it needs for its thriving about as much moisture as will be found in a marsh. And the thick old thatch is warm in winter, however much damp it may hold, and in summer it is the coolest roof there can be. Corrugated iron is gradually covering the world; and this is deadly hot in summer, and always noisy. But besides these obvious disadvantages of corrugated iron compared with thatch, corrugated iron makes one man's house look just the same as the next man's; while thatch ages and mellows according to the storms and the years, and the length of time since it was last repaired.

And so it gives to each man's house some different look from the next, which is the way that men are made, different from one another; whereas machines are the same, by the hundred, and wearily the same are the things they make, by the million. And where any possession of man's reflects his way or his whims, he must feeel as he looks at it that he is the master; but, when he looks at any of the myriad work of machines, he may not reason it out like this, but cannot help being aware with a feeling deeper than reason that it is the machine that is master here. Perhaps after the day of dictators the machine will be proclaimed in many cities as paramount; and in those days I think that the Irishman's talent for rebellion will make him the last to give in to the new unnatural tyranny. As this thought passed through my mind, out came my friend the farmer, a man with a good black beard, a beard among the last of those that the mongers of razor-blades have not yet advertised off men's faces. He came out with the genial air that I always saw about him, an air that seemed to conceal that he was doing a favor to me, and that seemed to pretend that I was favoring his snipe, by preventing them from being too many and so crowding each other. All this he more or less expressed in words, when I asked his permission to shoot his bog once more.

"What way is the wind?" I asked. For that is important in snipe shooting.

"Partly north," he said.

"It seems in the south," I said, "by the smoke of your chimney." For just then I noticed that from a wooden box on his roof the smoke was blowing nearly away from the sun.

"Aye, it's partly south," he said.

And so it was. Soon I was walking down wind along the stretch of marshes that lay along either side of a small stream, marshes that are called the "black bog" to distinguish them from the real Irish bog, the great expanses of heather that lie further west. It was in the dark of the moon, and the snipe would mostly be away from the red bogs, where they go to feed on a worm when the moon is full. The luring of the worm by the moon up from the deeps of the red bog is one of the many things that we know nothing about. No doubt it is quite as strong as the lure of gold with us.

One walks down wind on the snipe, instead of the way one approaches all other game, because he always likes to fly against the wind. So that, instead of flying away straight from you, he soon turns to left or right with a white flash, in order to get into the wind. He is a better mark then for many reasons, firstly because he does not get so far away in the time, secondly because his length is a bigger mark than his breadth, thirdly because the white flash of his side is easily seen against the dull rushes; and on the red bog, where all is dark and the snipe flies low, the flash of the white is particularly helpful. Lying dead on the ground he is usually not white, but, as with most birds, the feathers of his back closely resemble acres of his surroundings; and to give the eye a chance of marking him it is a good thing for at least one man not to blink after the snipe has dropped, but to continue to stare at the same spot until he is within five yards of it. After that the finding of the snipe is work for a nose.

It is essential not to speak when looking for snipe; scent is the principal warning to most animals, but to the snipe the human voice is the most definite proof of the presence of the enemy. Over and over again I have heard an ill-advised remark followed at once by the screech of rising snipe, and the flash of them going away, before one has come within shot. They seem almost more afraid of it than of the sound of a gun.

Some say snipe cannot smell. But they certainly breathe; and they must know quite as much of the flavor of air as we do. Therefore I am inclined to think that it is a mistake to smoke, when going down wind on snipe; even if one never smokes at all while shooting.

I could not tell of Ireland, without a word on

the snipe: London without the sparrow would be
a picture with lesser gaps in it.

Sometimes a snipe, that has been shot and been
gathered, is brought home and cooked for ten minutes, or even a quarter of an hour; even for twenty
minutes, for all I know. Then it is brown like
well-cooked beef, but not nearly so good to eat, and
it would have been better to let him live. Five
minutes are quite enough. Then the snipe is like
the food that gourmets are given when they have
been good to the poor and, with their gluttony
pardoned, have gone to Heaven.

Were I to tell of the snipe and not mention the
jack-snipe, the omission would be so invidious that
I might be thought by some to have a personal
grudge against the smaller bird, probably due to
my having missed him so often. The jack-snipe
rises without any cry, and waits till danger is much
closer than does his larger relation, whose relation-
ship is a much more distant thing than one might
suppose from their having the same family name.
He flies not quite so fast and with the apparent intention of making no twists; so that he seems a very
easy bird to shoot. But just as one is going to
shoot, he leaves his very gradual curve and goes
off on another; and, though his twists are far less
sudden than those of the snipe, his ways are de-
.ceptive enough for him to be very easily missed,
apart from there probably being room for him at

forty yards to fly through the middle of a charge of shot. He has long bright feathers, gayer than those of the "full snipe"; indeed there are more differences than resemblances between them; the resemblances being that they live in the same kind of country and get their food in the same way, with a long beak searching for worms down in the ooze.

Probably due to his beak being shorter and softer, the jack-snipe is oft to be met on even boggier ground than the common snipe; yet, in making any statement, one has to beware of illusion, and though I have met with the jack-snipe nearly always just where the bog was becoming most difficult, this may only have been because the bigger snipe that may have been there in equal numbers were all away, as their habit is, before one got near, and before the bog all round began to shake with one's footsteps.

This small bird is a great wanderer. One does not see him much before mid-December; and, when one does see him, one knows that the migration is come, and the foreign snipe are in. Half the common snipe that we see in Ireland, and nearly all the jack-snipe, nest far away in the North, and come to us rather later than the woodcock, which are said to prefer to travel by the full moon of November. I will tell a story about a jack-snipe, as I have known the same thing happen twice, and it warns sportsmen how they may possibly

waste their time. But it tells you something more
than that; it tells how two men may both be sure
they are right, and have good reason for being
sure; and all the reasons are very sound, except
that one of the two must be wrong. I had shot a
jack-snipe and marked it well enough and showed
my keeper where it fell, and he was looking for it
with a Labrador retriever, one of the best I ever
had.

The dog searched and searched till the rushes
were all trodden down. Perhaps we were there a
quarter of an hour. The time had long since come
when my keeper was sure that, if I had not missed
the snipe, it had come to life again and flown away
unperceived. He never thinks this at first, and
will take my word for it that the bird is dead, for
nearly ten minutes. But he was thinking it reso-
lutely now. And I was sure that the bird was
there. He said that the dog would never have left
it. He was as sure of his dog as I was sure of my
gun. What had happened? And then the dog was
quietly sick. And that explained everything. The
jack-snipe is so small a bird that this one had
slipped accidentally down his throat. Not inten-
tionally; he would no more have done that than
my gamekeeper would have done it. And I once
saw it happen in a river, when a dog was swim-
ming with a jack in his mouth, and the same thing
occurred; only that that time, if I rightly remem-

ber, the bird stayed there for good. As for deliberate eating, I once knew that happen too. But that was done by a dog that lived as it were in the twilight between this world and romance.

For it was a dog called Maria, told of in *The Experiences of an Irish R.M.;* and it turned out to be a real dog, as well as a character famous in fiction, or at least it was real on a day about thirty-five years ago when I was on a visit shooting near Skibereen with neighbors of the owner of that dog. It was a spaniel, and we were all looking for a snipe that someone had shot, and Maria found it and ate it. And I remembered how thrilled I was to meet even a dog out of that famous book. It is perhaps hard on my publisher to say it, but the bare fact remains that readers will get more of Ireland from that book than from anything I can tell them. But, alas, it is an Ireland, too much of which, someone has muddled away.

But I was telling how I went to shoot snipe in some marshes. We walked them all the morning, with the wind behind me; and I made a bag of snipe. How many they were I do not tell the reader, for he would give no thanks to Heaven because of it. They were not many. When I came back to the road the farmer was at his door, admiring the morning and waiting to hear what I had shot. I told him my small total of snipe and jacks.

"Ah, glory be to God," he said.

IX

Woodcock

PARTRIDGES are rare with us in Meath, where we grow beef rather than corn; and the pheasant is rather a dull bird to the sportsman. So I will not write about either of them. Yet the pheasant is by no means dull to the eye, as I was reminded when sending a brace to one of my tenants and finding when next I visited that house that the larder was thought altogether unworthy of such gorgeous birds. They stood in a glass case in the parlor. The woodcock is a bird far worthier of a sportsman, for his coming depends not on temporal things, like a check to a poulterer, but on powers that can grip man as well as the woodcock: the north wind and the cold. You do not depend for the woodcock on anything you can control, but on some fierce favorable wind and the full moon and the winter.

And if the number of woodcocks' eggs is affected by men at all, it is not by some poulterer in any city, but hungry Russians along the Arctic Circle, or Laplanders, or I know not what northern men, who may be taking their eggs; or so a bad year for woodcock may sometimes be accounted for. Or

sometimes one's speculations guess a storm, rising
up on the wrong night and striking the birds on
their journey.   And however wide of the truth
these speculations be, how far better it is to consult
some weatherwise old man about the chances of the
woodcock's arrival than to study the price of eggs
in any list. We do not know much of these flights
from the far North to Ireland. Dead birds lying
about lighthouses may give a clue to the man who
would spy as a detective upon Nature; but it is
only a clue. An airman told me that at 12,000 feet
he had seen a rook, a woodcock and a swan; but
two travelers passing each other in lonely places do
not often know where the other is going. And then
there is the heavy drag of the air at extreme
heights, lagging behind the spin of the world eastwards, which means a wind always blowing at a
hundred miles an hour the opposite way of the
world. That may help these strange journeys.

One Irishman who had lived half his life in
Yorkshire and had then come back to Ireland, and
who had shot at least one woodcock a year for sixty
years, told me that the woodcock were always in
when you heard about Shadrach, Meshach and
Abednego in the Lesson. But that was Yorkshire
lore and may not apply to Ireland. One may get
some clue to their coming by watching other birds,
birds that move by day and are more easily seen,
for I have never seen a flight of woodcock in my

life. When the geese move inland in their traveling formation, like the barbed head of an arrow, there are storms somewhere that have moved them, or great cold, and winter is coming southwards. What spring is to the poet, or summer to the cricketer, winter is to the sportsman. He waits for what the storms of that season will send him, and in a very humble way has a certain remote familiarity with the four great winds and the snow, such as the habitual onlooker at test matches comes to have with famous cricketers.

And whether his prognostications, or those of the weatherwise old men he consults, are right or wrong he comes to feel he has some part in the mystery of the march of the seasons round the world, and their servants the moon and the storms. Forerunners of these mighty things, the seasons and tempests, are also the golden plover; they will move at a touch of frost and go southwards or to the sea, mimicking in their flight the marching order of that great people the geese. When they move southwards it may also be a sign that the splendor of winter is becoming too arduous, and that the woodcock will soon be here.

When the flight has safely stolen into the country, past the full moon over the sea, we may still have to look for them without finding many; for, if they move southward from winter faster than winter can follow, they will go to the gorse and the

heather, or make themselves comfortable in rushy
fields or in ditches, till a frown comes into the sky
and winter overtakes them. Then with the first
fall of snow they go to the big woods, to sit on the
southern side of the trunk of a good tree, or under
the branches of spruce, that do for them what
slates do for us, turning white and silent with snow,
and letting none of it through. For, however su-
perior we are to the woodcock, we have like him
the job of keeping ourselves warm. Possibly, if
we could meet as disembodied spirits, far from our
present prejudices and preferences, and could discuss the matter, we might admit that the woodcock's way of keeping warm, with a big trunk to
the north of him and his feathers puffed out, and
the storm rushing angrily by him a few inches
away, was more exciting than ours. Possibly the
spirit of the woodcock would not change, even if
the change is allowed, his shelter of timber and
branches or couch of moss, for our fires and our
easy chairs and our bell to ring for more coal.
And perhaps if we offered those comforts of ours
in exchange, we might see the contempt of a spirit
that had known the north wind close, for those who
had heard it rarely and as a stranger. This seems
to me likely enough, though some may find it too
fanciful. But those who do not care for fanciful
things have no reason to read about Ireland.

The woodcock leaves the wood in search of food

as furtively as he arrived in the country. Men sitting for duck, or walking late in quiet fields, may see a dark shape flit by at the end of the gloaming, and that rarely; and that is all one sees of the woodcock's evening journey. Men who have seen badgers may see the woodcock flighting, and tinkers camping in lanes; but many a man's life-time may pass away without seeing the woodcock once. For he does not fly about like other birds by day, and is only seen then by those who drive him out of his haunts. One learns at first the places that are likely to hold a woodcock, always supposing that his vehicle has duly arrived, the north wind or the snow; and in the course of years one may come to learn the line that he will probably fly from any particular piece of covert.

For there seem to be highways and bypaths of the air by which birds prefer to travel, just as in wide fields the careful eye may notice that animals do not cross them anywhere, but travel by little tracks. Standing on the same spot from which I shot my first woodcock, I have twice got a right and left at them. As I have not very often got a right and left at woodcock at all, this would indicate that the trees, and the air-currents made by their shapes, would be favorable just there to aerial traffic. The color of a woodcock varies; either because they have in them some of the quality of the chameleon, and change their color after living awhile amongst bracken or dead leaves, until they resemble one of these things exactly, or because a woodcock of certain coloring goes to ground that resembles it.

Whichever way it be, a woodcock lying on the ground is invisible; and, in addition to that, his scent is not easily picked up by a dog. Having been picked up, he can be spoiled as the snipe can be spoiled, by over-cooking, though perhaps not quite so completely. If the legs are broken off at the knees before the woodcock are brought to the larder, the sinews are thereby loosened, and they say that the bird is tenderer. Those to whom the woodcock is rare may keep his pin-feather, a very delicate feather to be found under the rudimentary wing that emerges at the joint of the real wing. I do not keep them myself, but I never fail to be cheered when, in a town or anywhere far from woods, I see a solemn and urban bowler hat brightened by one of these tiny but unmistakable feathers showing above the hat-band. I feel then that

As an Arab wandereth in a waste of Ayaman

he probably does not expect to meet another Arab, on account of Ayaman not being on the map; yet, if he does, he must know some of that unexpected pleasure that comes to me when on pavement or near the wastes of it I meet a man with the woodcock's feather.

Though I have certainly never shown any gratitude to the woodcock, I am grateful to him for the romance of his great journeys, which add a thrill to sport. It is the same with the wild geese, and all these wanderers: they seem to bring the ends of the earth nearer; or rather, though leaving them infinitely remote, they bring their mystery nearer, till the splendor of Arctic mountains and Northern Lights are things at which our imaginations can peer, as they might otherwise never do, were they not awoken from sleep by the call in the sky that the geese make high in a wind going triumphing southwards; or the sudden notes that a magical shepherd might draw from a hidden flute, which teach that the golden plover are moving inland from storms. Once by a camp-fire in Africa a man told me how, near where we then were, he had been called from his tent by his gun-bearer and saw a herd of elephants going by in the moonlight, quite silently, and evidently making some great journey. I felt, as I heard that story, as I do when I learn that the woodcock are in, or I hear the geese going over; it is as though for a moment we had a surreptitious glimpse of the affairs of Nature, great enterprises closely in touch with winds and seasons and moonlight, beside which our undertakings appear narrow and local.

If one's imagination can sometimes follow a bit of the flight of woodcock or geese, and admire their starry journeys, it must seem inconsistent to shoot them. But if Ireland gave me the imagination, Ireland made me a sportsman. It is not consistency that we have from the ages, but impulses rolling up, sometimes from remote places, and drifting us this way and that.

X

Gray Lags

PERHAPS there is no better condiment to flavor
sport, or any other occupation of man, than variety;
and a well-mixed bag is always more attractive to
me than an even heavier bag all filled with the
same bird. Moreover the ultimate object of shooting is food; and, if one only shot one kind of bird,
one could not have it for dinner every day of the
winter, as one does where there is sufficient variety.
The golden plover is one of the birds that may help
to bring variety to the larder almost at any time;
for one may come on him in tame green fields,
lying outside woods when one is after woodcock or
pheasants, or one may hear the sudden whirr of a
flock of them sweeping over, when walking in
wilder country after snipe.

Or, at the end of a day, one may lie out on a
piece of waterproof in a field and wait for their
flighting. But to know the field that they come to;
that is the difficulty. I knew such a field once, but
another man got to know it too, and the golden
plover left it years ago. And then for a short while
I knew another such field; but it was close to a
town, and I did not go there very often before the

news that the golden plover came there for their flighting spread. I remember the large arc-lights in the town twinkling out as the evening faded. Far from spoiling the beauty of twilight and the feeling of hush on the earth, which always comes with this hour, those lights a few fields away only intensified the pleasure I felt at being alone with the evening.

Only a few fields away was the system that holds us all in stronger or weaker grip—the urban system, orderliness and regularity, that reaches far out into every countryside; but the hunter of anything feels that he does not belong to it. The poet makes his escape from systems too; but every kind of hunter is right outside it; his art began before cities. Watching the beauty of twilight glimmering in the sky and enjoying the contrast of all the things it enchanted, with the town whose lights were twinkling, I waited to hear the flute-like note of the plover or the whirr of their rapid wings. It was the hour when they should come, and as almost always seems to happen when waiting for any animal, from tigers to golden plover, one went on waiting after the hour at which one had thought they would come. All the small birds were home, and the rooks had gone over, and still no golden plover.

And all of a sudden at last I heard their note and even the whirr of their wings, but they were going over as high as traveling geese. Not long passed then, and they came back again. And all of a sudden they dipped, and out of the sky they came down like a waterfall, and soon poured over a hedge and into the field where I was. They raced past me not within shot, and wheeled and came back again. When they came over the hedge again at the same spot and went by on the same line, as though they were following an aerial race-course, I decided it was time to move, although moving one's ground is not always a good thing, and when done at the edge of night is usually bad.

I got up and ran, and lay down at a spot they had passed over. And I got there in time, and they came round once again. And I got two shots as their white forms flashed by me. I think that to watch birds falling out of a flock of golden plover requires a quicker eye than what is needed to shoot them; for I have often seen men, who were good enough with a gun, unable to see more than one bird drop, when there might be two or three. And another difficulty there is in picking up golden plover at evening; and that is that the grass looks so bright and clear that it seems that one can easily spare two or three minutes to get another shot or two before picking the birds up. And the three minutes drag on to five or six, and night is suddenly down amongst the blades of grass, where the golden plover are hard enough to see even by daylight.

The golden plover is not green, and neither is grass in winter; but the yellow glint of wintry grass in the sunlight and the dark shadows amongst the blades of it are imitated in a golden plover's plumage exactly. It took me some time to gather the birds, or to have them gathered for me by the retriever that my gamekeeper brought into the field when I whistled; and as we looked for them the night shrilled again and again with the notes of wandering flocks of golden plover that pass up and down in their aerial dances before they rest for the night. The electric lamps of the town glared now against the calm of the darkness.

And then there is sitting for duck. When it is cold and getting dark, and sometimes even snowing, one would never go out of doors were it not for sport. And how much one would have missed if one had not seen, out where one seems alone with it, the sunset turning the sky to a glory of colors, till the gloaming dwindles away and the stars are suddenly there. Or the soft pat, pat of the snow, and the gentle touch of the flakes, like the cold small hand of the ghost of an elfin thing. One would not have missed that either. Nor the cry of a strong wind's rage when it roars from the north, and brings the duck in low and drowns the sound of one's shooting. Or quiet evenings when winds go sighing faintly over the bog and whisper once to the rushes and are quite silent again, and the quiet dim glow of the sky is quiet and dim in the water, and the bog-rail croaks and croaks and no other sound is heard. Far away from the dry land the bell of a chapel tolls, and all is silent again. Again the bog-rail, and again complete silence. Then a wafting of air is heard and rooks go over, on their way to dry land and trees. The singing birds, with their little giddy flight, wavering up and down, have long gone by to their hedges. On such a night as that, quiet and still, I was out on a bog a few years ago with my gamekeeper. First of all in a ragged wood of firs, on the last of the dry land, I had waited for pigeons and shot one or two. But as soon as the air began to get mysterious, and the light had the look of a hand held up to say Hush, I walked out into the bog in my favorite suit of clothes, which is waterproof and fastens over the shoulders. It is made for fishermen, but is well suited to that particular bog. There must be places in it at which one might go over one's head, for a herdsman whose house in the fields was the last one saw on the way once warned me that in parts it was bottomless; which was an exaggerated description, but not an impractical one, for, when you are over your head, what interest have you any more in a foothold? I came to some little islands on which low bog-myrtle grew.

And on one of these I chose a place for myself, and lay down facing the west. One prefers to face west on these occasions, because one can see to shoot in that direction after night is behind one, and on one's left and right. Sometimes then one sees splendors of sunsets unknown in cities, splendors that often enough we miss even out in the country. And the light by which I wanted to shoot was fading with all its glories, while I waited alone with the bog-rail. The rooks on their long journey were gone, and the little singing birds that sometimes cross the bog were all home to their hedges; and then some green plover went reeling by with their uncouth gait, so unlike the arrowy flight of the golden plover and looking very black in what was left of the light. And then nothing came for a long while. It was geese I was waiting for.

The evening star appeared. And very soon after that I heard the slow quack of the first duck to arrive, and even the whirr of its wings; but I did not see it, for it was on the dark side of me, to the east. More came and went down in the bog, and I could hear them quacking on the water. Once in the dark that was now closing down on the bog I heard the quick small whistle of several teal. Then there was silence again; a silence on which the bog-rail intruded once, and then left it unbroken. There was a long silence then, and the light was slowly fading. And then I heard the first note of the geese away in the northwest. And suddenly they all broke out into their jubilant outcry, and soon after that I saw them coming towards me, in a long line and coming low. There must have been more than thirty of them, gray lags. The little islands to which I had come were where the geese had been before, and they seemed to be coming very nearly straight for them. They were to the north of me now and the light was bad, and I missed with my right barrel and fired again as they passed. And they disappeared in the dark, and I heard the thump that is made by a falling goose coming down on a still night. The first thing I did was to tie my handkerchief to a bit of bog-myrtle that grew on the little island where I was. Without this the bog could hide all one's bearings, like fancies lost to one's memory. Then I went to find my gamekeeper; and he and I and the dog looked for the goose. It was the dog that found him in the dark, and a fine effort it is for a retriever to drag a gray lag over the bog. We came away, all three of us very pleased, to the dry land, steering by lights with which little windows far off were cheering the cold and the loneliness. And we came to a road, with my goose, where a motor was waiting for us. It was a fine plump goose and we talked a good deal of him, though I have no memory of what we said. But these words I seem to remember, when we got home, at the end of our conversation:

"I wouldn't say anything about all those men that we saw, and we coming away from the bog."

"I didn't see any," I said.

XI

Business

"ARE you coming out tomorrow?" said a friend to me, for the hounds were to be within five miles of me.

"No," I said. "I am writing a book about Ireland, and want to get on with it."

"About Ireland," he said. "What are you telling them?"

"Oh, sport," I said, "and poetry and history, and of course politics. But not much history, for the book is to be in one volume, and that volume is to be lifted with one hand."

"Another reason why much history would be out of place in a book about Ireland," he said, "is that they none of them know any of it."

"I thought it was one of the things the people are fondest of," I said.

"They are," said he, "but in the schools, where they learn it, it is only used as missiles to throw at England, so that it gets rather tattered. It is very exciting of course, but you couldn't any longer call it history, after it has been the round of a few schools."

"Well, I don't know very much about it myself," I said.

"No, nobody does," he replied. "But you're right to give them sport; and I think there's some poetry in all of them."

"Their talk is full of it," I answered, "and all their legends."

"Yes," he said. "But what are you doing about politics?"

And then I told him about Old Mickey, and how there was one thing that everybody would want to know and Old Mickey was going to tell it me.

"Yes, you'll have to tell them that," he said. "But what about business? You should say something of that."

"Oh, yes," I said, "I suppose I should."

But the remark rather bothered me, we haven't very much business in County Meath. We used to sell fat cattle before the treaty and got £35 a head. We still sell fat cattle; but, as we only get from £12 to £14 a head for them, one can hardly call that business.

"What business is there?" I asked.

"Well, there's Guinness," he said. "And there's bound to be some more somewhere, if only you look for it. Anyway you'll have to have something about it in your book."

We were both agreed about that. And I decided

to make further inquiries, and with the help of them to study the matter locally.

And by good luck I met next day just the kind of man that I wanted, a man whose kindness had helped me to get many a teal; for he had not only showed me a reedy pond to which the teal came, but many a time he had driven them for me, telling me just where to hide myself and seeming to know exactly the line that the teal would fly. He was an old friend of mine, who had known a good deal of prison in his youth; and the imprisonment, while gaining him the respect of all his neighbors, had never impaired his cheerfulness. Now that the words will soon be in cold print I begin to realize that to know the flight of teal is not in itself sufficient qualification for knowledge about business, and that there may even be amongst my readers some that will hold that before venturing to address them upon this matter I should have found an adviser with better qualifications. That may be so; indeed it is incontrovertible; and I should certainly have done so. On the other hand I was not at once able to find a man with the better qualifications, and I was undoubtedly hindered in my search for one by a certain charm that there was in Stephen O'Lara, who now stood before me, and who would, I believe, have exerted the same misleading charm on the most critical of my readers; but that, of course, I cannot prove. I had found

him a good deal occupied watching a river. It
was a bright morning, and he was leaning over a
bridge and did not recognize me till I spoke to him.
Then he jumped up, all smiles.

"I was watching the river," he said, "and didn't
see you."

"It's a fine day to be doing it," said I.

"Begob," he said, "it must take a long time to
get to the sea, the pace it's going now."

"It gets there all right," I said.

"I was wondering did it ever get there," he
answered.

"How is the country doing?" I asked.

"Sure, it's doing grand," he said.

"And how is business doing?" I asked.

"Business is it?" said he.

"Well, yes," I said. "I rather wanted to make a
study of it."

"Sure it's doing grand too," said O'Lara. "They
are after opening a great new bank over at Bohermeen."

"At Bohermeen?" I said.

"Aye," he said, "to the west of the road."

It was the kind of thing that I wanted to know.

"That's the road to Fahan," I asked, so as to
make no mistake.

"Aye, three or four hundred yards from the
crossroads," he said.

"When did they build it?" I asked.

"They're just after finishing it," he said.

"Who is the manager?"

"The honestest man in all Ireland," he said.

And then he told me this rather interesting story.

"Pat had a bit of an army of young lads down in the West, no more nor about half a dozen. He wasn't the general himself, but there was another lad over him. And one day he went into the big bank that there is down there, and asked to see the manager. And the manager came out of his office, all business and buttons, and said: 'What can I do for you?'

"And the young lads put up their pistols, and Pat said: 'I want £4000.'

"And the manager said: 'I haven't got it.'

"And Pat said: 'Then you've not long to live.'

"And the manager said: 'I might scrape it together.'

"And he did.

"'Can I put it into some bags for you?' said the manager.

"'You need not,' said Pat. 'Do you think I am going about with all that money on me? Sure, I wouldn't be able to walk.'

"'I thought you wanted to take it away,' said the manager.

"'Have more sense,' said Pat.

"'Then what do you want to do with it?' he asked.

" 'Sure, I'll bank it,' said Pat.

" 'Where?' said the manager.

" 'With you. Why not?' said Pat. 'You can put it to my account.'

" 'I'll want a specimen of your signature,' said the manager.

" 'There'll be no difficulty about that,' said Pat. For they had learned him to write. So he wrote down his signature, and they all walked away; and Pat turned his head round, as he was going out, in the doorway, and said: 'Is there a priest handy?'

"And the manager said: 'There is.'

" 'Because,' said Pat, 'if ever I come here for the money and don't find it, you'll want him in a great hurry.'

"With that he went away, and there was £4000 to his credit in the bank. Am I tiring you?"

"You are not," I said. "What happened?"

"Well, a few weeks went by and then the general that I told you about, who was over Pat, died one night from the prod of a cow's horn. I knew the doctor who attended him, and he told me that that was what he died of. It went through the whole length of his body. 'It must have been a very long horn,' said the doctor to me, 'and a very thin one. But that was not my affair.' Well, when Pat heard the general was dead, and being a queer fellow and the honestest man in Ireland, what's he do but go back to the manager of the bank and give him back his £4000. Yes, he done that. He did indeed. And when they wanted an honest man to run a bank, what did they do only get Pat? And where could they have got a better? For he knew a little about banking, through having had an account of his own, and he was dead honest. And it's a true story I'm telling you."

"I want nothing but the truth," I said, "for I'm writing a book about Ireland."

"It's God's truth," he said.

And then I left him to look at the river, while I went home to write about business.

But when I got home I decided that I had best first go and see Bohermeen, and have a talk with the manager of the new bank.

So when my gamekeeper came to see me next morning to ask me where I would shoot, I told him that I couldn't shoot that day, as I had some business to attend to and wanted to see the manager of the bank at Bohermeen.

"I never heard of a bank at Bohermeen," he said.

"No. It's a new one," said I.

"But it would be a grand place for snipe," he said, "and there's none of the men with rights in the bog who will object to your going there."

"Well, I'll take my gun," I said, "and we'll bring the dog, and I might get some shooting when I've finished the business I have to do."

But I said no more of the bank; for, though I

valued his opinions on sport, I did not think that
he had sufficiently accurate knowledge of business
to justify me in basing upon his opinion on banking the information about business in Ireland that
I desire to give to my reader. And soon we were
off, with dog and gun in the car, to Bohermeen,
which lies northwest from Tara. One cannot see
from the famous hill the low levels to which I
went, but very clearly one can see the Hill of
Fahan, against whose feet laps the heather of
Bohermeen. I have seen the Hill of Fahan from
Tara at evening, with its wood on top turning ruby,
till the gap that there is in the wood becomes like a
gateway of Fairyland. The low steep hill in the
plain is one of the principal landmarks of the
country. We came to Klimessan hill, where the
land dips to the west, and we saw Meath and Westmeath lying blue before us. We crossed the Boyne,
and went through lands of green pastures, till we
came to little fields of coarser grass, which very
soon ceased altogether, and we came to the lower
levels of the bog, that men have plundered but not
yet tamed. A few young birches stood there, that
men had planted in rows along ditches that they
had dug, and some turf-stacks stood there drying;
but there was nothing else on those levels that told
of the work of man. A road ran very lonely over
the bog, looking almost shy of its own sophistication amongst ancient primitive nature. And then

another road ran away to the right. So narrow was
this one that it seemed almost to slink over the bog,
like a man in patent-leather boots, tall hat and
frock coat going on tiptoe through an encampment
of gipsies, knowing he had no business there. This
was the road we followed, till I came to the exact
spot of which O'Lara had told me. The low levels
of the cut-away bog had ended before I came there
and the long black cliff lay before us at the edge
of the high bog, its outline jagged by the turf-
cutters. It was two hundred yards past this that
O'Lara had told me I should come on the new
bank. I stopped the car, and the distance seemed
about right and I should have been standing just
about at the doorway. But no bank was there,
nothing but pale brown grasses, with patches of
heather amongst them, and a view over bog unbroken but for one dark row of pines to the left-
hand side of the view and a small wood to the right,
and some mountains that are in Westmeath rising
beyond it. Behind me on the other side of the road
lay the lower levels with patches of whitish grass
and patches of moss, and square pools shining; I
saw a loose donkey there, and one in a cart, and
two men standing by turf-stacks. I looked again
over the bog, and away to those mountains in Westmeath, but the only sign of sophistication I saw was
one broken bottle, that had been thrown to the bog
from the road; but certainly no bank. Had I been

content to write about the Ireland I know, instead of wishing to instruct my reader about whatever business may be done in the country, I should not have been out on this wild-goose-chase. Let the metaphor pass: I know of no more unsuitable one by which to describe a search for a bank; but let it pass.

"We'd better shoot snipe," I said to my keeper. And that is what we did.

I was rather annoyed with O'Lara for sending me off on this absurd quest, when it was solid information I wanted; so I went a little out of my way, coming back, so as to find O'Lara. And I found him, where I usually find him, not far from the Boyne; and he seemed as pleased as ever to see me, and seemed to know, too, where I was coming from, and looked as though he were happy to have provided me with just the information I wanted. I seemed to see all that in his smile. But all I said to him by way of greeting was:

"There is no bank at Bohermeen."

"Ah," he replied, "perhaps it was a turf-bank I meant."

"You told me," I said, though my annoyance was melting before his smiling face as I spoke, "that there was a particularly honest man as manager there, and I went all the way to have a talk with him."

"Sure, everything I told you about him was

true," said O'Lara. "Doesn't the whole country know it? And what for do you want his right address? Wouldn't the story about him be just as true whatever address I gave you? Begob, it would. And maybe the wrong address might be better. But, sure, I'll find him for you and bring him to see you."

"It doesn't matter," I said.

"What was it you wanted him for?" said O'Lara.

"I wanted to have a talk with him about business," I said. "I'm writing a book about Ireland, and they'll want to know what business the country does."

"Haven't we Guinness?" said he. "And what do we want with any more business than that? Don't they pay millions in taxes?"

And then a troubled look came over his face.

"Begob," he said, "I've nearly given up drinking it."

"Why's that?" I gasped.

"Because of a dream I had," said O'Lara, "after drinking no more nor a bottle. And then I went to bed and I had the dream."

"What was the dream?" I asked.

"Begob," said he, "it was terrible. I dreamed that I walked down to the shore of the sea one evening; I don't know what I was doing there, but I walked down to the shore; and it was somewhere near Dublin, for I could see the Wicklow mountains. And it wasn't night, for there was still some light in the sky; but it was getting late. And the shore was crowded with people all looking out to sea. And I said, 'What's the matter, boys?' And one or two of them answered, 'It is the end,' and went on looking out to sea. So I looked too, in my dream. And I saw the horizon all dark with the smoke of ships, and the people staring at them as though the end of the world were there. Begob, I said to myself, it's the English fleet, and those great big shells will be coming soon.

"For the smoke was tearing up and the sky was black as thunder.

" 'Is it the English fleet?' I said.

"But they had all gone silent, and wouldn't speak any more.

"And then I saw that the ships were nearer than they looked in the evening. They weren't far away at all, and were quite small. And I took a man by the arm who was standing quite near me and I shook him, and said, 'Those little boats can't hurt us; sure, they're no bigger than Guinness' boats that do be on the Liffy.'

"And the man gave a great sigh and said, 'It is what they are.'

"And I cried out then, 'Ah, boys, is it Guiness's going?'

"And I knew from the awful stillness that this was so.

"And I daren't have a sup of porter before going to bed any more, for fear would I get that dream."

"Oh, I wouldn't bother," I said. "It was only a dream."

For he looked so doleful, I had to say something to try to cheer him.

"It isn't the dream I mind," he said, "but all the truth that there is in it."

NEWTOWN ABBEY ON THE BOYNE, WITH THE KEEP OF TRIM CASTLE ON THE HORIZON

OFF FOR A HUNT WITH HORSES AND HOUNDS

XII

John Watson

The thought comes to me to make a claim for Ireland, that the people of other countries, should these words ever come to their eyes, are not likely to allow; for it is to claim that we have more personalities, per head, than they have in other parts of the disunited Kingdom. And that is a claim to a part of Heaven's wealth. As oaks grow best in wide clearings so personalities probably best thrive far from cities, and unaffected by the influences that cities throw out to great distances round them. These influences may be summed up as tending to orderliness and to sameness, while personality has other ingredients. Personality in Ireland is limited to no class, nor could I point to any class in Ireland that tended to produce more personalities than another.

Looking back at the forceful men that I have known, my memories come first to John Watson, Master of the Meath Hounds. It is hard to define personality and hard even to analyze how one has been impressed by one: the thing is probably a combination of the work a man does and the character that he puts into the doing of it. John Wat-

son was not only a master of hounds but he was
also a huntsman and a field-master, three jobs not
frequently undertaken by one man, and all three
done by John Watson consummately. A man may
be a fine huntsman and yet kill few foxes, if he is
not a good field-master or has not one to control
his field for him. A few enthusiastic riders riding
over the line, and occasionally heading the fox,
will spoil any hunt.

But John Watson's imposing figure, his fine
voice, and his tremendous language, awed his field,
who obeyed him just as his hounds did. Polite and
pleasant as he was off a horse, on hunting days he
spared neither age nor sex. But I must be strictly
accurate, remembering that I am making the attempt to describe Ireland and the Irish people:
there was one lady with whom he never found
fault, whatever she did, the Honorable Mrs. Dew-
hurst. She won his lifelong respect like this: one
day many many years ago, she or her horse having
exceeded the length to which he felt his field ought
to go, he turned to her and said, "Woman! Go
home."

She did not obey; but turned to him and said,
"Go home yourself, you damned son of a bald-
headed Carlow onion."

John Watson never forgot it, and never ad-
dressed a cross word to her again.

I remember one wet day when a lady jumped on

one of John Watson's hounds. He was annoyed, and said so; though I don't remember his words. And then he drew the covert blank, outside which this episode had occurred. And it was raining all the time, and the rain went on. And he drew another covert blank. And still the rain fell. All that day John Watson drew coverts blank, and all day long it rained. And when the last covert was drawn, John Watson turned to the lady in the rain, and we realized then that during all that bad day he must have been brooding on what she had done, for he called out to her, hours after her unintentional offense: "My good woman! Next time you hunt with my hounds, I'll ask you not to do so in the middle of them."

I remember noticing that day that I was really wet to the skin, and that the water was running along it, only as I rode in at my gate; till then the good cloth of a hunting-coat had kept out anything more than mere damp.

It was a large country that John Watson hunted; there must have been a thousand square miles in it; and he hunted it five days a week. On the odd day, that was Wednesday, he used to go out with the Ward Stag-hounds, a hard-riding hunt that gives to the inhabitants of Dublin, its suburbs and neighborhood, a sight of the hills of Meath and the plain of Kildare. So hard-riding a hunt are they that a story is told, and passed on again as worth telling, how once a man out with the Ward who had jumped on another rode back to apologize. His horse was hard to hold and it took him some while to stop him and turn him back from the hunt. But he did turn back, and rode back to apologize. And the man who had been jumped on was just getting on to his feet, and the other man's horse was still hard to hold, and he knocked him down again.

All the summer John Watson played polo. He never rested; and at last he wore himself out.

Once when I was playing cricket for the Phoenix Park Cricket Club on their lovely ground, near enough to the Dublin mountains to see the whole range of them clear, and far enough to see the smile on their faces that they only let you see at a certain distance, I walked away during our innings and came to the edge of a crowd that was watching a game of polo.

"Who is playing?" I asked of a friend that I met as I came up.

"John Watson," he said.

"Who else?" I asked.

"Well, I don't know them," he said, "but I heard John Watson saying 'Damn you, Dick' and 'God blast you, Jimmy' and 'Hell take you, Ned,' and you may know who they are."

Once, riding a horse that was not too easy to hold, and a good hundred yards behind John Watson, I saw him come to a gap in a hedge, growing,

as all Meath hedges grow, on the brink of a good
ditch; and I supposed he was going to take it at a
gallop, but he checked and took it slowly, and by
the time he jumped I was nearly on top of him.
I said nothing, for the enormity was too great for
explanation. And for once *he* said almost nothing.
He had a kind heart in him, and I was very young,
and his forbearance was very likely due to pure
kindness. But I thought at the time that he was
so astonished that he, of all men, should be jostled
by anybody, that his mighty flow of words deserted
him utterly. What he did say I remember to this
day, after more than thirty years: his exact words
were: "Well! Well!"

To tell of those days when John Watson was
hunting the Meath would, I think, be to write the
history of the Golden Age in Ireland. Is that because the cattle trade was still flourishing then? Or
because during some of those years Lord Dudley
ruled, an open-handed sportsman, remembered
yet? Or because the Wyndham Act had satisfied
Irish tenants? Or because Dublin was still a city
with something of an air, and a thriving trade?
Or was it because I was young? Can the impartial
historian's conclusions ever, I wonder, be sifted
and separated from his own personal views, and
from all the little things by which they were
formed? One cannot be sure. I had better ask
somebody else. So of almost the first man I met in

a field, as I was coming up from a bog next day,
where I had been shooting snipe, I inquired of this
very thing.

"It's a fine day," I said.

"It is, glory be to God," said he.

"A fine soft day," I said.

"It is, sure," he answered.

"Do you remember the days," I asked, "when
Mr. John Watson was hunting the Meath, and
Lord Dudley was Lord-Lieutenant?"

"I do indeed," he answered. "Sure, who'd ever
forget them?"

"We've had a lot of changes since then," said I
without committing myself.

"Ah, God be with the old days," he said.

I see that I have not been able to write anything
to show, to those that did not know him, the personality of John Watson. His ghost will not walk
in these pages, nor has he a place in history; but in
the minds of many hunting-men he lives on still,
a giant among their memories; and there are old
sportsmen sleeping in chairs at their firesides who,
if you shouted to them, "John Watson wants to
know what the hell you are doing there," would
hastily back their chairs away from the fire as they
waked.

XIII

The State of the Moon

I HAD not intended to say anything of astronomy;
but Irishmen watch the heavens as well as other
people, and only the other day in a letter from a
friend I read a tale of the moon that sufficiently
interested me for me to hope that it might interest
my readers also. There may be scientists in England who will disagree with the lunar investiga-
tions told of therein and they have every right to
do so; only let them not state that they know more
about such matters than Irishmen do, for that sort
of thing does not go down in Ireland. The letter
was from a lady, recording a talk between a man
unnamed, and a workman on the shore of the mouth
of a river. "Well, Tom," said this man, "how is
the country going on?"

"The country!" said Tom. "Is it *that* you're
asking me, your Honor? What way could it be
going, with all the salaried Inspectors walking
around the roads with their boots polished and a
gold pen sticking out of their pockets and the day's
newspaper in the hand reading about the danno
fighting and the killing and all the murdering they

do be doing in foreign parts, and not a day's work to trouble them?

"Sure the country's capsized with their likes, and don't you well know it yourself, sir. Sure the poor old moon can't do her work no longer. Look the way the tides be, that weak no stir in them at all! Sure she's dying like the rest of us. She was great in her day! Swinging the tides up the river, and the fishes lepping to be up first. But these new rules and regulations and the likes, have sickened the life out of her. Poor old moon, I feel sorry for her. For she knows the country's capsized, and she's dying."

I repeat this conversation, verbatim as I received it, only for its astronomical value. I mean no criticism of any government officials; for I believe that Tom would never have minded them walking along the roads, or having their boots polished, or possessing gold pens, if only they had not been reading about murder in foreign parts; and it was unjust of him to grudge them this little luxury which cost no tax-payer anything. And I make no comment on the effect of politics on the moon, because a faith in the power of politics has been until recently, and may be still, a faith much cherished in Ireland; and to deny its power for evil might be to deny its power for good, and I should not like to do this while anyone in Ireland still held to the old belief.

I was writing in the last chapter of a great personality, and I mentioned that personality in Ireland is not confined to any class. I should think that Tom of the river-mouth, with his wide observation of heaven and earth, and his abundant power of expression, was one of these personalities; but I cannot say, for I never knew him. I have had the good fortune, however, to know many such, some for a lifetime or the best part of it, others for moments as we passed on a road and exchanged greetings or fragments of philosophy or fancy. I knew once a man that was known as the King of the Wreckers, who lived in the middle of Meath and was supposed to hold some sort of authority over all whose avocation was to help men and horses fallen in ditches while following the Meath Hounds or the Ward. Others would greet one with the words: "Do you remember the day when I found you in the big ditch over beyont Lagore? Begob, your bay horse would be in it yet but for me."

It wasn't true, but they got a shilling.

But the King of the Wreckers seldom spoke: there was a great calm about him, and you felt that even half a crown was barely sufficient for the price of a drink, when he was the man that would drink it. And there was no reason for giving him any money at all, yet you felt it was due to him;

that feeling was part of the aura that shone from his personality.

And there was a man who cost me much more than the King of the Wreckers, for he used to seek me out, while the other I only met at meets that were within a comfortable walk of his main address. He would come to my door and say how well I was looking, and I would give him a shilling or two; and he would grow very confidential and speak in a rather low voice, but full of intensity, and say to me: "I will tell you how it is. It's like this. Listen now, and I'll tell you. This is the way it is." And then with emphasis all threaded with mystery: "Two shillings would be no good to me."

"No," I would say. "I see."

And he would shake his head over it, seeming to ponder as he shook it, upon the wisdom and truth of what he had uttered. His right to be helped was so taken for granted, and his statement that two shillings would be no help was so earnestly made, that I really used to feel glad if I could get out of it for less than ten shillings. He is gone now, and my purse is the better for his going; but I feel that the neighborhood is poorer for the loss of something that I cannot define, and will therefore write of no more.

And now, as I pause to remember what other personalities I have known, it occurs to me suddenly that they are all personalities; all of them, that is to say, looking at life from their own point of view and expressing what they see in their own way; and it is that that enriches their talk with poetry, fancy and wit, and even wisdom, and that that makes them impossible to govern. A nation needs such people, a few dozen of them, to run its arts and see its visions, and even sometimes to lead the rest; but, when it comes to government, the fewer there are with a taste for making their own laws, the easier will government be. And this thought leads me to digress for a moment from Ireland, out to the larger world, and to remark that the whole art of good government is to strike the best balance between the authority of the Crown and the liberty of the individual. If the balance swing too far towards authority, everyone is apt to be uncomfortable: if it swing too far away from it, a good many are likely to be starved or slaughtered.

But let us return to Ireland to search for personalities, which will be an easy task once we have recognized that nearly every Irish man and woman is dowered with this possession. It is not the spread of knowledge that stifles personality, but the organization that spreads it; so that, if you were to ask the opinion of a wayfarer about anything met by the road, in any country where knowledge was properly organized, you would be likely to get the same opinion as your own and expressed in your own phrases. In Ireland you would get a new opinion. You may say that it would not be as good as yours: but that is not quite the point; the point is variety. If you gazed intently at a drop of dew without moving you might know that the light in it was red or green; and yet if, in spite of your knowledge, you asked someone standing beside you, he might tell you that it was violet. It is good to look at the world in the same way, helped by other views of it from other angles.

What examples shall I instance? Here is one. Once at the edge of a bog on a cold winter's day I offered a man with whom I had got into conversation some whisky in a tumbler, that I had brought in my car for just such a need as his on such a day; and it happened to be pre-war whisky, or at any rate rather good. How should one express one's respect for fairly good whisky? In many lands such things, no doubt, are all laid down by custom. But this Irishman expressed his respect for this whisky in his own particular way. At the first sip he went down on his knees, and remained kneeling until he had emptied the tumbler.

It is a curious thing, personality: it so flavors all a man's acts, that you can trace him by any one of them, almost as you can by his handwriting. I met an instance of that only recently: I was talking to an American about a man I had known when he lived in Ireland, though he was not Irish by birth, and I mentioned the man's name. "I knew a man of that name in New York," said my American friend, "he used to paint and play the flute. I wonder if he was the same man."

"I don't think he ever painted," I said; "and I never heard him play the flute. I don't think it could have been him."

"And he brought a cow to the hotel in which he was staying. He wanted to take it up to his room in the lift."

"A cow in a lift!" I said. "The very man! It must have been him."

And really I don't know now what made me so sure. But I was sure. I felt that no other man would want to put a cow in a lift; and that it was just what this man would have done. Though I had never seen him with a cow.

I suppose personality is what makes one man different from the next, as a goat is different from a herd of a thousand sheep.

I wrote the last chapter or so of this in England, and now I am back in Ireland again, and winter is hovering. Bleak and raw and cold as the dawn can be, coming up over Kingstown, it is always pleasant to arrive in Ireland. There is a certain softness in the air, even in winter, as though the air were robed in a delicate dress made out of threads of rain and a myriad dewdrops, woven together by magic. There is a magic too in the people and the kindly welcome. Oh, the grace with which two porters received their sixpence each for wishing me good morning. I did not see at the time, and I scarcely see now, that they had done nothing for me or the morning: I only noticed that they took their trifling pay with no ungenerous suggestion or hint whatever that it was in the least inadequate. Through the almost silent town and through Dublin we drove, and all the houses were awaking from sleep; only the gulls, on our right, were already awake. I like to see houses waking; by day they are merely houses; but, just emerging from the mystery of night, all flashing with dawn that only they seem to see, and twinkling within with one candle, like an old man over a thought, they seem to stand just halfway between things that we think we know, and the mysteries that night shares with inanimate things. Thin plumes go up from their chimneys into the sky, and soon they are all awake, and the light grows bright till the mystery is very nearly gone. We have come from London at the end of November, when the great city sits brooding under her ancient cloak, which is fog, and not much sunlight will disturb her aged thoughts for another month or so. But the country is all bright in November, and to that brightness is added a flash from the few remaining leaves, and one looks out of the windows of the car eager for some of the sights that the country has to show, and which one has not seen for awhile. Unfortunately that same fog has reached a bit wider than usual and lies white all over these islands, in addition to which a frost is turning it into two sheets of ice as it touches the two front windows of our car.

When one comes to a railway one deduces by those methods with which Sherlock Holmes was wont to astonish Watson that a train has passed that way, for smoke floats heavily for as far as one can see; but how long ago it was that the train went by is more than one can tell, for all smoke that goes into the air today, and even the breath of cattle, lie in the air like ghosts that nothing is able to exorcise. And so one comes home with familiar landmarks leaping out of the mist, and with nothing at all in between. A priest walks slowly to his parochial house from saying early mass and no one else as yet seems to be about at all, except such as have business with cattle and are walking slowly towards Dublin. Soon we were welcomed by hundreds of banners waving behind a wide smile: all the banners were the tail of one dog, and the smile was warm and wet and full of ivory. We were back again, and I have no further need of letters such as I quoted earlier in this chapter, as material for this book; for now I can get all such comments upon earth or moon as I may require, from the people living all round me.

XIV

Swans

THERE was good news for me when I got back, news of the discovery of a red bog of which I did not know, about fifteen miles from here, where the owners would hospitably allow me to shoot. And news of a new red bog was particularly welcome to me, for the moon is nearing its full, and all who follow the avocation of snipe-shooting look at that time to the red bogs. London without cats would be far less unlike the London that is, than an Ireland without snipe would be unlike the Ireland we know. And in this Ireland a tide of snipe goes backwards and forwards, drawn by the moon, invisibly, probably by night, from the red bogs, which is where the heather grows upon deep morass, to the black bogs where there are rushes. When the moon is full the snipe go to the red bogs, and few are left at the bottoms of valleys or by marshy edges of fields; and when the moon dominates the night no longer, back they go to the other marshes, to the lands that are called the black bogs, which though sometimes very deep are never of peat. They say that the moon lures up a worm in the red bogs, and that these worms come to the surface to gaze on the full moon, and that all the snipe go to find them. Those of us who ever make far journeys, and those who read of travel in which there is any romance or adventure, are probably inclined to be so dazzled by the doings of man that they overlook that his most adventurous journeys are equaled by all kinds of animals. This pilgrimage of the snipe to the red bog, by night, at the fall of the moon, has always seemed to me a mysterious event. You go to the marshes where they have been for a month, and find scarcely any there; and no one has seen them go.

If the frost lasts there will be no snipe on any red bog, for the surface will be like rock, and their bills will be unable to pierce it. We must look instead by the streams. And this I did, but not very energetically, for sleep on the train cannot always be counted on, and in St. George's Channel the boat seemed troubled by fog, and the mournful note of her foghorn was rather disturbing to sleep. That night, looking out after dinner, I saw clouds piled high and keeping the earth warm, and the wind had changed, so that I had the feeling that the white frost on the grass would be gone by morning.

Gone sure enough it had, and I was soon back to the familiar marshes again. The snipe had returned, though not yet in great numbers: there were only five on the first small bog that I came to, and by a great piece of good luck I got them all. Then further afield, and on the way back, while waiting for snipe to be driven across a lane, I had the luck to meet an old fellow called Hurricane Jim, though I never knew how it was that he came by his name. And, after a brief talk about snipe, he generously advised me to go and look for them on land that belonged to neither of us. I shall not go, but I thanked him, for his interest in sport was genuine, as well as his intention to help me. I asked him before we parted if the golden plover were in, for he walks the roads a great deal and would have been sure to know. But he thought I meant the green plover. They come together, or about the same time, though the golden plover leave earlier than the green; so his information was useful to me.

"They are not in it," he said. "They are late this year. I don't know what has happened them. And I am lonesome without their calling."

On the way home we came on a string of hay-carts, that many a motorist would have cursed, for only the foremost one had a man looking after it; yet it was part of the life of Ireland, if one was not in too much of a hurry to notice it, hay cut far away near the larger bogs on the western side of the county, on their way to the Dublin market. Those men from the edge of the bogs would sleep that night at Clonee, having done over twenty

miles, and with eight more miles to go. Early
next morning they would be in Dublin, about the
time that townsmen awake.

Another day came, and the grass was all white;
for the frost was back, just when I wanted it least.
It is one day before the full moon, and I had meant
to shoot the new red bog, but the frost is there
instead. A little later, and the bird that Ireland
knows so well, the woodcock, would be in the
coverts sheltering from the cold; but their passage
is only booked for tomorrow night, if lore that is
handed down the ages from mouth to mouth may
be trusted, and I know not what else to trust when
inquiring of ancient things like the flight of the
woodcock. So it is no use beating the coverts for
the two or three home-bred birds that one might
find in them now. And they are better where they
are. For if you were thinking of taking a house,
and saw one in which no one lived, not even a care-
taker, there would be something about it that
would never attract you, as would a house that is
properly cared for. It is probably the same with
the woodcock, and they are likelier to come to a
wood in which one or two of them are, than to what
must look to a woodcock a homeless wood.

The only place that I could think of for any sport
today was a reach of the Boyne above Trim; and
there I went, and it looked as if the snipe had gone
to the red bog after all, for I only got just enough

for dinner. It may be worth while recording a
very simple aid to securing snipe when shooting
along a river; but simple things are very often the
best things, and can be overlooked. The simple
device I speak of is to have a handful of stones in
one's pocket, for a snipe is a small object in the
water, and, if one's dog does not see it at once,
the current may very soon carry the snipe away.
One had best take round stones, avoiding angular
ones and flat ones, the angular ones because they
might cut holes in one's pocket, and the flat ones
because they may go sailing away through the air
and fall nowhere near the snipe. Any object
thrown on land would only confuse a retriever,
and so would a stick in the river; but a stone sinks
as it marks the spot, and the dog goes straight for
the splash, and if one has thrown straight and
allowed a bit for the current, that should bring
him near enough to the snipe for him to do the rest
for himself. A teal is a far harder job, unless it is
quite dead; and a winged teal, once in the water,
is not much easier for the dog to get than a fish.
Only one of my snipe on this occasion dropped in
the water, and was easily gathered, as well as those
that dropped on the dry land. I always take a
towel in the motor with me on these occasions, and
a complete change of clothes; the first for the dog
when he has been in a river, and the second in case
I should make an injudicious step in a bog.

It is a good thing to have no exceptions about the spare suit of clothes, even when one is going to the most innocent marshes, and then whenever the soil that floats on water gives way and lets one through, it will not be on a day when somebody thought that one could not possibly need a change of clothes today. Were it not for this precaution there might be some professional walker of the roads tramping them now in breeches splendid with darnings of different colored wools: as it is, I keep them for myself. And very welcome they are, on the rare occasions when I get in over my knees. The habit of carrying this old suit in the car whenever I go shooting I have had for about thirty years, since the time when I needed it unexpectedly and had to borrow another man's at the first cottage I came to.

It was a small and innocent-looking bog, but a good many tufts of heather might have warned me that it had once been a red bog that had all been cut away for fuel. The cuttings were old, and long overgrown, though not long enough overgrown to hold my weight, and I went to my neck with the suddenness of the cessation of music when they are playing musical chairs. My request for a change of clothes when I got to the cottage was immediately granted, but was thought to be inadequate, and I was pressed to have whisky too, the argument being that "it had saved many a life." I

drank the whisky and was the better for it, though
the remark of my hospitable neighbor set up a
train of thought as to the relative numbers that
whisky had saved and killed. I do not know what
I was doing on the bog on that day at all, for I
remember that there was a thin film of ice on the
moss and the water, so that there cannot have been
many snipe there; but I was younger and less ex-
perienced and more hopeful then.

The cold and the northerly trend of the faint uncertain wind, and everything that spoiled my snipe-
shooting today have driven southwards the green
plover at last, and the golden plover with them;
for I saw a few of both in the fields today: and once
or twice a small black cloud went swiftly over the
lower part of the sky, which was the golden plover
traveling. Any night now the geese may come into
the country, and even that queer but unmistakable
note of musical wings may be heard, as a pair of
swans go over. Some fiercer rigor, far north, has
come into the mood of Winter, and the golden
plover upon those pointed and rapid wings have
brought us the first news of it. By walls where the
fields end, and in cottages out amongst them, the
news that the birds bring is interpreted, more
keenly than ever it is in the great cities, more keenly
if not so accurately as where they are wont to rely
on the announcements of science; but working out
for oneself information that one has had at first

hand from nature, as though Dame Nature herself had brought the news to one's doors, is a pleasanter thing, surely, than reading any announcement. If anyone says it is not, I should like to see someone else blurting out the whole of the crossword on which the first man is working, and to note whether the bald statement amuse him at all.

And better than reading the weather forecast in print, and almost as good as trying to work it out for oneself, is to consult some wise old man whose wisdom is never from books and rarely finds its way into them; for there is a certain savor to news which one gets that way that is scarce to be found in print. The news of the coming storms, or whatever it be, may be mixed up with folklore, such as prophecies founded on berries, and it may be even tainted with legend or magic; but even gold is rarely found raw, unmixed with other fragments of Mother Earth; nor is it impossible to strain the gold out of quartz, or ample truth out of legend. Swans are spared in Ireland by every man with a gun, on account of their beauty; but I do not think that in every case the sense of the swan's beauty is pure in the man's mind, unalloyed by legend, and some remembrance of the Children of Lir or other heroes that had the misfortune of being turned into swans by magic may reach from myth right through history, down the ages, to secure mercy for swans.

Perhaps for the benefit of those that do not know
Ireland I should explain how it was that Lir's
children came to be swans. The Children of Lir
were three sons and a daughter, and Lir was a king,
or would have been but for Bov the Red who had
been proclaimed lawful King of Ireland; but Lir
did not set much store by that. So Lir lived in
rebellion awhile. But eventually he married Bov's
daughter Eva, and the three sons and the daughter
were their children. Then Eva died, and Lir
married again, another daughter of Bov the Red.
And this daughter, whose name was Aoife, was
fond of her sister's children, but turned after a
while into the ordinary stepmother of legend.
Growing tired of her stepchildren she turned them
into swans by magic, much practised by all her
people, the de Danaans. It was on Lough Derravaragh that she did it, having first of all told the
children to swim in the lake and then working the
witchcraft on them.

The four swans, which they instantly became,
remonstrated with Aoife and asked her at least to
decree some end to her spell. This she agreed to
do, and sentenced them to three hundred years as
swans upon Derravaragh, and three hundred years
in the Straits of Moyle between Ireland and Scot-
land, and three hundred years in the seas by Erris
and Inishglory, after which the enchantment would
end. Then, as an Irishman selling a horse gives

back something when the bargain is over, she allowed them to keep their human speech and to sing sad and unequaled music, and to keep their human minds.

It was not very wise of her, for, of course, they gave her away to Lir, who told it to Bov the Red, who could do magic himself as well as any of them, and smote Aoife with a wand of the druids, who flew shrieking from the hall and became a Demon of the Air, and is one still. "All the high sorrows of the world" were in the music of the Children of Lir; and three hundred years went by, and Bov the Red and Lir were still hale and hearty, and the time came for the swans to leave Lough Derravaragh. It was then that they came, as they were bound by the magic to come, to the Straits of Moyle, and there they fared ill in bitter nights of January and outlived many storms, while Lir and all the de Danaans were holding the Festival of the Age of Youth, which meant that by magical means they were escaping old age and trouble. And the de Danaans knew that the Children would be freed from the magical curse "in the end of time."

And there came the end of the second three hundred years, and the four swans rose and went from the tides of Moyle and, leaving behind them the cold of that stormy sea, they flew to Inishglory. And there they dwelt for a while. But when the

end of time came, or at any rate the end of nine
hundred years, they arose from Inishglory and flew
to find the palace of their father, which was on the
Hill of the White Field. But they found it desolate and thorny, with nothing but green mounds
showing where the palace and halls had been, and
nettles growing thick over the mounds. It must
have looked very much to them as Tara looks to us.
And then they knew that "the old times and things
had passed away in Erin, and they were lonely in
a land of strangers." For they did not know that
Lir and all the de Danaans dwelt on invisible in
the fairy mounds.

They had not yet taken human shape again; but
one of St. Patrick's men named St. Mochaovog
came to the land of Inishglory, and began to say
matins and to ring his bell. The bell frightened
the swans at first, but soon they realized that the
bell was a holy bell, and that it should deliver
them. And the end of it was that one day their
feathers fell off, and the three princes and the
princess stood there shrunken and withered with
age. And the princess said to St. Mochaovog:
"Come and baptize us quickly, for the end is near."

And Mochaovog baptized them, and soon they
died, and were buried as Christians are; but their
graves, with one in front of the princess and one
on her left and right, seem rather to be placed on
the lines of a flight of swans.

Those who ask of a legend the hard and fast question, is it true or untrue, would probably miss a great deal that the ages have learned in Ireland about the migration of swans. Many a time I have seen inlets of the sea where the legend places Moyle, beautiful with white flocks of swans, and the feathers of them lying along the sand. People that watched their movements probably made this story, and only diverged from truth by trying to tell two stories at the same time, and mixing up natural history with the story of some woman who was jealous of her stepchildren some centuries before history shook itself free from legend and learned to look after itself.

Lough Derravaragh lies under a small steep hill that I can see from any high part of my own land, and I know its actual shores, for it is near to the home of good friends of mine. So Derravaragh is actually there; but it has never emerged from legend, and probably never will; for many legends cluster thickly about it. As I have mentioned it, I had better tell of its origin, which was this. The witch of Westmeath sent to the witch of Galway to borrow her lake, saying that she would send it back on Monday. So the witch of Galway rolled up her lake and sent it over the hills to Westmeath, and the witch of Westmeath unrolled it at Derravaragh; the proof of all this being that there is a lake at Derravaragh, and a hole in Galway of the same size and shape. But it did not end there; for the witch of Galway asked for her lake back, pointing out that the witch of Westmeath had promised to return it on Monday; but the witch of Westmeath had replied that she meant the Monday after eternity, or Monday-come-never. So the lake is still at Derravaragh, as anybody can see.

And the legends that haunt it have not done haunting it yet; for there is a family to which Derravaragh is unlucky, and one day some of the members of it decided to go and row on its waters. Whether they knew or not of the evil influence of the waters of Derravaragh upon their family, their old dairymaid knew it, and all the people round, for it was one of those old families in which the Irish people take a great interest. The dairymaid warned them, and then besought them not to go. But in the end they went, leaving her almost tearful. It was a hot summer's day with thunder about, which may have added to the feeling of doom in the air which was felt by the dairymaid. And then they came back safe. Almost the first words that one of them said on returning were said to the old dairymaid: "You see nothing happened to us."

But she looked at them full of knowledge of dooms they had overlooked: "No, but the cream turned," she said.

XV

A Bit of Philosophy Strays into the Wrong Book

THE sun went down last night red and curious, turning the last of the leaves to pure gold, and calling up huge wraiths of towering mist from all the low-lying country. And, as might have been feared from this, a frost came in the night; and today is the full of the moon, and the new red bog waiting. We decided to try it in spite of the frost, and on a bright clear day it was a fine sight to see. And this authentic Irish soil is a good thing to walk on, compared with pavements, which I have lately trod. And there is a welcome for most people beside Irish bogs, whereas in towns, where everybody nowadays is dressed all alike, no one knows who the next man is, and they are inclined to suspect and hate each other. This may seem a strong statement.

Let me therefore tell a ghastly story. In an *Evening News* of this month of November, 1936, I read a statement that had been made in court by a representative of a London railway company. "All who buy tickets," he said, "from our automatic machines come under suspicion, and may be

149

followed." This statement tallies with observations of my own. Thank God there are none of these damnable automatic machines round here.

One advantage I must concede to pavement, and that is that there are no bog-holes in it. The bog that I went to today had been a good deal cut, and a small cutting covered with heather takes almost more watching than one can spare from the snipe. Bog-holes today were more numerous than snipe, and I got no more than about one snipe a mile, and found one bog-hole for myself, but luckily with only one leg, for the fall forward usually brings one on to a firm patch of heather. A frost having spoiled the bog, we turned homewards, getting a curlew on the way, and a few more snipe by the edge of a river. And tonight the mist has risen up into tall shapes under a gorgeous western sky, to prophesy more frost. And tomorrow is Sunday, when the weather will little concern me. I might have been seen this afternoon driving a cow slowly across a field, to which some golden plover had come. In spite of the name on the cover of this book, it was not my cow. The cow minded little, and its kind owner not at all. And as happens, as often as not, when in quest of golden plover, I did not get a shot, for they had moved to the next field; and the curlew was the bird in the hand, and the golden plover escaped. The frost was very light; and, had it been any harder, the golden plover would have been away to the sea. There are not very many in yet, and we shall want more storms in the north before more of them come. Bullocks may also be driven, to bring one within shot of golden plover, but driving a bullock for this purpose is a very difficult job, for he is always trying to turn to the left and then to the right, in order to gallop back to the herd, or may start to gallop forward just at the wrong moment.

The moon is perfectly round, but is wearing a woolly halo that is suggestive of fog. If fog is lying over much of the world tonight there will be no flight of the woodcock, for such lore as I have been able to gather from my neighbors tells that birds never flight in fog. The frost is white on the grass again, so that the feet of rabbits, when one opens the door to look at it, can be heard a long way off, making more noise on the grass and the frozen leaves than a tiger does in his jungle. Snipe, golden plover and the full moon may seem trivial things to write about; but then I am writing about a rural land, and sport is to the countryside what business is to the cities; and though the following of either gets one far afield from one's starting point, yet one gets far farther with sport, for he who would put his wits against those of the wild creatures must know something of things that they know, and learn the way of the winds and the frost and the moon. But now there returns to my

mind a thing that I had momentarily forgotten;
and that is that when I came in sight of the bog today and looked out over all its colors, I saw a
woman in a red dress coming out of it with a pail
of water towards her cottage. That red dress in a
bright morning added so much color to the bog that
all artists would have delighted in it; and, as it remains a beautiful thing in my memory, I will pass
it on, though dimly, to my readers.

It is Sunday now, and fog and frost are gone;
and if the old saws be true, the woodcock crossed
last night. Henceforth, when the frost or snow
comes to the bogs, I can turn to the woods to follow
that occupation that was my principal interest
before ever I took to writing, and that the world
for that matter followed long before Homer—the
pursuit of game. The running of tram-cars may
be more interesting to some, or banking or buying
or selling, but the rather queer title that stands at
the top of these pages must debar the reader from
these. And now it is Sunday, as I have said, and
I have not even sport to tell of. I will tell instead
of things inside the house. And first I will tell a
tale told me today at lunch, for it illustrates very
well the courtesies that there must be when two
well-ordered camps are pitched side by side; not
camps of hostile armies, for the two churches in
Ireland are both Christian, but two corps stimu-
lated by rivalry and perhaps a little jealous of

each other. They will fight none the worse for
that, side by side, when the trumpets call to Armageddon. But of the strategy of Armageddon I
must say nothing, for that is the affair of holier
folk than me. Well then, at a certain house, one of
the most beautiful in this county, a clergyman of
the Church of Ireland and a Roman Catholic priest
were both of them guests at luncheon. Their
hostess hesitated for a moment before deciding
which of them she should ask to say grace. Rome
won, with courtesy and with wit, though not without a light shot fired at heresy; for her priest turned
to the other, a model, I may add, of perfect
sobriety, saying: "You say grace before lunch, for
I am quite sure you will not be able to say it after."
    The lady who told this story, which reached me
today secondhand, is I hope an old enough friend
not to grudge my bringing it thus to the eyes of
some who may not know Ireland, for the sake of the
light it may lend to them. Other stories, too, I
heard today at lunch, but I will not repeat them,
as I promised earlier in this book not to be telling
Irish stories, unless with good reason; for that is
too easily done, and one may easily drift into telling tales that are merely amusing, without as it
were focusing the light of their humor on some
particular trait of the Irish character, or condition
of Irish life. Nor am I going to give an inventory
of my house, though I remain within its walls

nearly all Sunday; but one thing caught my eye to-day, preserved here in Ireland from ages whose wisdom this age has forgotten, and its lesson is such a good one that I will tell of it. It is a piece of carved wood to hold a barometer, and the carving shows Diana standing under a tree, with stags and boars and hares at her feet, a spear in her hand and her horn at her side and the ends of her arrows showing; an appropriate ornament for a case to hold a barometer. But that is not the lesson: the lesson is that the barometer is turned to the wall, and Diana is outwards. If you want to see the barometer, you turn round the carved lady of myth and look at the mercury. All the barometers and thermometers that the present age possesses hang with their faces outwards; and those faces add nothing to the pleasantness of our outlook, nothing to the beauty of the world. The first thing that the earlier ages did was to set up walls and roof, as shelters against the rain, and the second was to soften what was ruggedest in the world in which men had to dwell, and to give the dreams and fancies of men dominion over the harsher and cruder things. You could see at a glance in those days that man held an important place on the earth. But now you would rather say that steel was the more important. Steel is shaped by man no doubt, but not to his dreams: man has only served steel as a slave. And so we have machinery pushing forward everywhere to a foremost place in the world, and the dreams and fancies of man are far behind. Ask a hundred people of the relative importance of a great machine or a work of art, and you will discover that most them put the machine first. The arts are made of human emotions; God knows what the machine is made of. Utility comes first everywhere. But what is utility, but an end that can be seen by even the most shortsighted? All the great ends lie further. And where is utility leading us? The answer to the question wholly depends on how well machinery serves man, or whether machinery serves man at all; whether it is friendly, neutral or hostile, or whether man merely serves the machine. Thus I philosophize, being idle, because it is Sunday and I have nothing to shoot.

XVI

Snipe

It is Sunday night, and the wind has changed; a matter that may seem too trivial to record; and yet the southwest wind which has come has brought back the Ireland that we all know best. It is our national wind, the wind that has made the Irish grass and the Irish character, that brings the moss on the southwest side of trees and bends the heads of all thorns, that are not well sheltered, over to the northeast. And with the southwest wind the frost is gone, and the soft air come back, and cloudy skies; and rooms at the back of the house are no longer scented with wood-smoke drifting in with fog from gardens that lie to the north of us. To-morrow should be a day to suit a trip to the red bog at last.

Tomorrow has come and the wind is still in the southwest, and the red bogs are all soft and their mosses waiting for snipe. I went to the new red bog again, and walked a good deal and got nine snipe, perhaps two a mile this time; but the frost, as my gamekeeper puts it, has spoiled the moon. A good many snipe returned last night to the red bogs, but while they should have been going there they were frozen out, so that some are on the red bogs and some are on the black, and nowhere is a big bag very likely to be made this full moon. But it was pleasant to be walking a bog again, even a difficult one, and this one has many little square holes cut in it by people who seem once to have taken from it a single barrowload of turf and never to have come back to dig at the same spot again. I often wonder how it is that one watches for snipe getting up on a bog, about forty yards ahead, and at the same time watches for a good foothold for each step. As I never remember how one does it, I cannot pass on the information to my reader. All one can say is that when one has time to spare to look at the ground one should avoid all bright mosses, while heather is always good to hold one, but should be watched to see that the spreading tops of it do not conceal a hole. In addition to little diggings for turf there are the hare-holes to be avoided; for while, perhaps a thousand years ago, men were digging pits for elephants in Africa, a similar school of thought was devising the same sort of method in Irish bogs for catching a hare. And a trap that is too subtle for such intelligence as is possessed by a hare is far too subtle for the average man.

It is a curious thing, but I know no large bog in this county that has not a small steep hill at one side of it, as though it were designed for watching the bog and seeing who might try to come across it, and, in the only exception I know, one has been built, that is to say a rath. It has been built by the side of the one road crossing the bog, which goes over the narrowest part of it and is probably as old as the rath. It must have been a fine position for an encampment, for whoever held it must have been safe from any attack from half the landscape, so long as one man watched whatever pass there was over the bog. As much history lies in these bogs as is in books, if one has the luck to find it; for every kind of implement that men ever handled in Ireland has sunk at one time or another into the bogs, and every now and then men digging for turf find the bronze heads of spears, and sometimes even gold. They are strangely preservative, these bogs, and men that have fallen into them have been found, clothes and all, as well preserved as the mummies of the Egyptians. Here also men used to bury kegs of butter in order to keep them fresh, or butter in earthenware jars; and I think that some glimpse of the yellow treasure, or some story of it that changed as it was passed on and on, may be the origin of the faith throughout Ireland that little men buried crocks of gold in the bog or at the roots of thorn trees.

Should my reader wish to look for one, the place to search for it is where a rainbow touches the earth. Thorn trees, I may say, are particularly

sacred to everything that is pre-Christian, and to
this day there are few men who would willingly
cut a lone thorn on a hill or out in a field, or one
showing by any queer twist of gnarled branches,
or grayness of age, that it is likely to be sacred to
those who were great in their day, before St.
Patrick came to trouble them, and who might not
quite be trusted to have lost their power yet. Anyway it is felt that it is better to leave such thorns
alone, for a great many things may happen that
you might not be able to be sure of, and maybe
there are things in the world that we don't all of
us know yet. And so in the middle of a plowed
field, with the furrows twisting round it, or in any
other unlikely place, old thorns may be seen standing; and, if any English traveler ask the reason
of it, he will be given as many reasons as courtesy
demands, and then a few more to spare, but not
the right one. I heard a story only today of a
farmer who was cutting one of these thorns; and
he had no faith in the Shee or any of the little
people; and the thorn tree fell suddenly and jabbed
a thorn through his hand as it fell; and the man
who told me the tale did not pretend to be able to
account for it. The force of gravity is one thing
to be considered. But it may well be argued,
"What cause would the force of gravity have to
harbor a grudge against any man? Whereas the
Shee . . ." But there is no saying what the Shee

might or might not do, if you went out of your way to injure one of their thorns; so thorns and Shee and all such things might be better left alone. Aye, that might be better for a man in the end.

Coming away from the bog I saw a windy thorn on a hill, standing alone where once men probably camped and watched the bog to see that no enemy crossed it. It leans to the northeast, where an age-old wind has bent it, and is not the sort of tree that anyone would venture to cut down. It has a wild look standing there, and wilder still seen from the bog; and, if the mind of whoever sees it be soaked in ancient legends, its gnarled trunk and clawing branches are just what they would expect. As a matter of fact a great deal of gold has been found just under its branches; found by some men and lost by others, for it is just above the point where the winning-post used to stand some years ago when the Meath used to hold its point-to-points there. So, many men have done the work of leprechauns under that thorn, putting down gold for others to find. Belief in the leprechaun is dwindling in Ireland now, though not the fond fancy that believed in him; that tends to be transferred to sweepstakes and politicians. Politicians do good to the country in lots of ways; and one of these days I am going out to look for that good, where a rainbow touches the ground.

Tuesday has come, and the wind still blows suitably for snipe, though it has wavered a bit from the point from which our Irish climate comes, and is a little too much in the west and not quite to be trusted not to bring bad weather. I motored past Trim, with its towers and spire and steeple standing up bright in clear sunshine, and came to a red bog, on which I hoped still to find snipe three days after the full moon. I walked the whole length of it, half of it high bog covered with heather, and half of it a plain, ten feet lower, where most of the turf has been cut away; I don't know how many thousand tons of it. Heather still grows on this plain; but on much of it red grass grows, and red mosses and bright green mosses. It was by these mosses I walked, where they went like long inlets of a lake amongst the heather, and at the other end of the bog I met my motor, which had been taken round to a road that ran by that side of the bog. We came back in the car, so as to have the wind behind us, and walked the bog again, and walked back over it this time to our original starting-point, though the wind was in our faces.

For that contrary Irish bird is best approached down wind, as one hunts no other game; the reason of this being that he prefers to fly up wind, so that when you come down wind on him he has to turn to get into the wind, and so gives you a crossing shot. For several reasons a crossing shot is the easier, provided that you aim far enough in front.

One of these reasons is that his more vulnerable
parts are exposed, and another is that he shows
white when turning, as he does not when going
straight away, and this against the dark of the
bog's surface is a consideration; and then again,
when his flight takes the form of a right angle, he
remains within shot longer than when he travels,
at his sixty miles an hour or so, in a straight line.
And lastly I walked across the width of the bog
at the western end, the end that the wind was coming from. Most of that part was also cut away and
it was mainly bright-red mosses floating on soft
deeps. Here and there the low black precipices
of the original peat stood crowned with heather,
above square pools of water in which green moss
floated slimily. The little turf-stacks dotted that
plain, and here and there some industrious worker
had entirely protected his stack of turf from the
rains of winter by clothing it with a light thatch
of rushes. These looked in the distance like little
houses of whoever might be wild enough to live
in that wild land. There were not a great many
snipe on the bog, for the lure of the moon seems
weakening, but luck and my dog's nose favored
me, and I got fifteen.

My reader will know that a great many good
racehorses come from the South of Ireland, but he
may not know how they come. Nor do I, for that
matter, for the method is recently changed; but I

heard this morning how some of them came until lately. I am giving no man's secret away, for it was no longer a secret when it reached me, and indeed a southern Irish policeman was one of the links in the chain of gossip, although not the link with which I connected. My reader, who will have often observed the gloss that shines on a race-horse, particularly when set off on a sunny day with bright colors in the saddle, will readily appreciate how much a little paint and a lot of mud and a tinker's cart will help to disguise these animals. Yes, some of the horses seen stepping daintily at important race-meetings have drawn a tinker's cart over the border from the Irish Free State into Northern Ireland. The tinker would harness up with a very old horse, and go back for more. I wonder how they go into the North of Ireland now.

XVII

Sitting for Duck

IN writing of *My Ireland* I have told of the southwest wind and the soft Irish air, but have said
nothing of the ether. Why should he? some may
say. But does any man quite know his own country nowadays? If singers with mandolins, or
traveling bands of musicians came every night to
one's door, in any land, and one were telling of
such a land, one would surely mention that. Tonight I have been listening to Spanish airs, showing
clearly old African origins: they came through the
ether, and wireless remains to me the greatest wonder in any land. What its influence will be on the
minds of civilized man I cannot say, but Europe
can no more be the same as it was without Marchese
Marconi, than it can ignore Julius Caesar. It may
become the enemy or the friend of ignorance; that
depends on how it is used. In the isolation of
lonely valleys something is gained and something
lost, as in the roar of cities also. Henceforth
neither walls nor mountains stand at the back of
concert-halls between the orchestra and the remot-
est people. One may write of Ireland, it may be
thought, well enough without digressing to wire-

less. But can one? Will old isolations remain the same? There are men in Ireland who never had heard Big Ben, who can hear it now any evening. And what effect will Big Ben have on them? I do not know. That is why I say that I cannot tell what the influence of wireless will be. Meanwhile the ether vibrates with it, and this mysterious power will dominate minds that barely know it as yet for a new plaything. Above the weather, between the earth and the stars, the voice of man, as mysterious as Northern Lights, goes wandering further than swallows.

And now Wednesday has come, and the west wind still blowing, and I went to shoot some small bogs, some of them among the first that I ever shot snipe on, and holding snipe still, for the ways of the bogs change less than our ways. I began with one called Ballynamona, a long narrow marsh under a hill. A causeway has been laid across it, to carry the weight of a cart. I remember once among the stones of this causeway finding the head of a gargoyle. I do not think there can ever have been a church in that marsh: more likely the stones were brought in carts from ruins far away, not that you need ever go very far in Ireland to meet with ruins. And then cartloads of stones were thrown down at the edge of the marsh, and further afield till they crossed it; and out of the heap of stones one day I found leering this old stone face. Light

rain came into the west wind, and Ballynamona
was not holding well. I came next to the Black
Cut, a bog in which it is not so easy to keep one's
knees dry, but always good for snipe. And then I
came to a place like a small pond, to which the
earth had come shyly back. There may have been
swans on it once, and lawns near it, and even a
house. One never knows. It is certainly something that had been excavated deep, and the earth,
that had covered the water, only uncertainly holds
one's weight. I shot six small bogs in all, and then
left them to the rain and came home with fifteen
snipe. A herd of cattle passed us as we were having lunch by the road, and another man looking at
the drover as he passed said to me: "I'd bet my
life that man knows his way over the border."

Long before this book is in print the drover will
have been over the border or not, or I would not
give him away; and, after all, the only evidence
adduced for this illegal knowledge on the part of
the drover was that he was "a sweet hearty cut of a
fellow."

One of these days I must remember to ask Old
Mickey about the destruction of our cattle-trade
in the South of Ireland, and see what he has to say
of it.

I will mention another simple thing that may be
of use to snipe-shooters, for though it is simple it
comes in very handy, and that is to carry a ball or

two of paper rolled up in one's pocket, to throw
down as a mark. It is better than throwing one's
handkerchief into the bog, and one probably only
has one of those. And in addition to a ball or two
of paper it is a very good thing to have an old
tennis ball, as one can throw that further, and in
any wind. But the tennis ball is likely to sink
down among the rushes and be lost; it is, therefore,
a good thing to tie a piece of tape to it, at least
a foot long, with a bunch of white paper at the end
of the tape. These precautions are not so necessary
when one only has one snipe down, but when one
gets a right and left one wants to mark the first one
as quickly as possible, and then get after the second; while, if one gets another snipe or two on the
way, it is very difficult to pick them all up without
these marks. A dog cannot search the whole bog
for one, especially as he may be often led astray
by the scent of live snipe that have flown off.
Sooner or later, too, that tempter of dogs the hare,
may run across the bog, and, though no good retriever would dream of chasing it, the scent is
strangely exciting.

And now there is a certain monotony in the
larder, which I hope to vary tomorrow when I go
to sit by a pond in a wood, to which my gamekeeper
has lured a flight of ducks. To lure ducks to a
pond is no easy work and the secrets of it are not
for all men, so I will give away no more of the

process than to repeat what my gamekeeper told me he told a man who asked him of it. "Chop motor tires up very small," he said, "and boil them a long time; and there's nothing that ducks like better." Those are his own words, which I merely pass on without comment.

The night is very dark and damp, and there seems no fear, as I look at it after dinner, of frost coming to spoil the flight.

Thursday has come, and I have had a hot lunch, instead of going to the larger snipe-bogs, for my designs today are chiefly against the ducks, though I visited a small marsh in the morning. When I returned I found a ballad-seller at the door, a man who walks the roads through the Irish weather, until one would think that some fragments of cyclones and anti-cyclones would be woven into his coat by now and be going round Ireland with him, and with him, too, go the Irish songs that he sells, printed on bits of green paper. I bought one for my readers; and the price would have been six-pence, but that, as the ballad-seller pointed out, it was getting so near Christmas, and I shouldn't be seeing him again before that, or indeed before Fairyhouse races. His ballads, the old wanderer told me, were printed in Ireland, but composed in England, so that I suppose that mass-production has overtaken even these, and very much machine-made they looked; but the one I chose was Irish, written, I was assured when about to buy it, by the greatest ballad-writer in all Ireland. Here it is, with two of its misprints corrected and without the dirt in its folds.

THE BARD OF ARMAGH

Oh! list to the strains of the poor Irish harper,
   And scorn not the strings from his poor withered
      hand
But remember his fingers oft moved faster,
   To raise up the memory of his dear native land.

'Twas long before the shamrock, our green isle's
      lovely emblem,
   Was crushed in its beauty 'neath the Saxon lion's
      paw,
I was called by the colleens around me assembling,
   Their bold Phelim Brady, the Bard of Armagh.

Ah, how I love to muse on the days of my boyhood,
   Tho' fourscore and three years had flitted since
      then,
Still it gives sweet reflection, as every young joy
      should
   For the merry-hearted boys make the best of old
      men.

At fair or at wake I would twist my shillelagh,
   Or dance the fine jig with my brogues bound
      with straw

And all the pretty colleens in village and valley,
  Loved the bold Phelim Brady, the Bard of
    Armagh.

Now tho' I have wandered this wide world over,
  Yet Ireland is my home and a parent to me,
Then oh let the turf that my old bones shall cover,
  Be cut from the ground that is trod by the free.

And when Sergeant Death in his cold arms shall
    embrace me,
  To lull me to sleep with sweet Erin-go-Bragh
By the side of my Kathleen my young wife Oh!
    lay me,
  Then forget Phelim Brady, the Bard of Armagh.

It is quite a good wind that is blowing now, as I
realize on looking up and seeing how few leaves
are left on the oaks, which were shining all golden
yesterday, and on the other trees none at all. The
wind will suit well for shooting ducks, for the
noise of it limits the distance at which the sound
of shots may warn those on their way, and in such
weather they seldom circle warily round, but come
in "like arrows." It is half past three, and the
light by now will be nearly gone in London, while
here there seems a slight fading in the glow of the
low clouds racing over the sky from the west, that
reminds me it will soon be time to have tea and
put on my boots and get started.

And so I motored down to the edge of the wood

in which the pond lies, and got a pigeon that was
just coming in, and walked down to the pond and
made myself comfortable on a wooden bench in a
"blind" made mainly of growing spruce, that were
planted for that purpose. Finches were flying
home when I came to the blind; and soon the wood
was ringing with some discussion of great importance to birds. The wind ran like a ghost over the
water, whitening it as it went. Clouds were so
low and thick as they hurried by that one only saw
the gaps in them moving, for through the gaps the
lucent dome of the sky gave the only light by
which to see clearly. Very soon the ducks came,
and very soon the light went. They came black
against the sky, sliding down the air over the tips
of the trees, and suddenly becoming invisible
against the dark of the wood. And as they enter
the dark of the trees they put their feet out and
draw in their wings a little, and drop rather than
fly, so that their pace is greatly altered just at the
critical moment.

It is no longer a matter of aiming a long way in
front; one aims instead a little way underneath.
Nor is it a shot that one can practise every night,
or ever in broad daylight. When my right barrel
was fired they would swoop over the surface of the
pond and rise again over the trees; and not till they
were over the trees could I see them again, and so
get a long shot with my left barrel. Soon the light

was quite gone, and I had got eleven. With two
dogs we picked them up, and for the last two or
three we used an acetylene lamp, but not till we
had got all we could without it, for dogs work
better without the glare. There is not far to go
through the wood on the way home, but the lamp
came in handy then, for, well though I think that
I know the wood, it is very easy to lose oneself in
it at night. Then we came to more ornamental
trees, growing nearer the house: the wind in their
branches was like a great voice. There rose the
rather pleasant sleepy smell of burning leaves, and
a small red fire winked at us. Then lighted windows in the night, and home to warm rooms and
away from the splendor of the wind.

XVIII

Golden Plover

Next day a few more snipe, and then a menac-
ing look on the face of the sun, that gave all the
west a thrill as it set over marshy country. And
one had the feeling that the bright air threatened
a change of weather, and that there might be on
their way those storms and cold that give a point
to the houses we build and a purpose to thatch and
good fireplaces; for it is against wild weather that
these things are designed. And next morning the
prophetic look had gone out of the sky and the cold
was already there and a wind from the west with
a bite in it. We set out by car for a large bog that
lies a few miles away, in a hollow of land that may
once have been all a lake. And on the way we met
the golden plover; not flocks of thirty or forty,
such as I have seen recently, but many hundreds.
They were massed in a field when we first saw
them; and soon they were up, but did not go very
far; and we planned a maneuver that almost
worked too well, for the golden plover came over
a hedge so close to me that my shot scarcely had
time to spread. However, I got four, and they
were in fine condition. And, as I was not very far

from a village, the shooting provided for one or
two people that sight of a bit of sport that is always
welcome to Irishmen; for, although the Irishman's
spirits should be sufficiently volatile to soar of their
own accord, he does like the occasional stimulants
of whisky, sport and politics. For choice he perhaps prefers all these three things refined and puri-
fied from any alloy of law, as for instance when the
whisky is poteen, brewed in a bog out of sight of
the law's representatives and paying no duty to
them. With the golden plover in the bag we
motored on to the nearest point that a road went
to the bog, and we walked down towards it against
a west wind with fury in it, I regretting the good
coat of sheepskins that I had left behind in the car,
and that is made in the mountains along the northwest frontier of India for just such weather as this.
"There is the real smell of winter in it," said my
gamekeeper. And sure enough there was.

As we got near the bog a cloud of dark blue rose
up on the far side of it, and we decided to take
shelter from the last bit of shelter that there was
on the dry land before going into the bog and meeting the storm that must soon come out of that
cloud. And very good shelter we found, a good
warm haystack. And had it not been for my Labrador retriever the cattle that were there sheltering
too, prevented from eating it by a strand of wire,
would not have grudged it to us. As it was, they

had to watch the dog, for to watch a dog whenever there is one in sight is a lore that is handed down among all cattle, from the times when they had to watch his cousins the wolves. Suddenly a line of white appeared over the bog, and a snowstorm came towards us. It did not last very long, and, as the ends of the dark cloud were raging away, we started on again and got to the far side of the bog with the wind behind us, which was a change after having it for some while in our faces, and, as I have said before, the best way to shoot snipe. Snipe were very scarce today and I only got four, but it was pleasant to walk that wild stretch of marshes so rarely trodden by man, through the pale brown reeds with all their pennons streaming the same way. And the dark plumed head of one of these reeds has to be watched very carefully whenever one drops a snipe. If it falls a long way off one must watch the dark-brown plume without ever blinking; for let the eye stray for an instant, and the rush that stands sentry over one's fallen snipe will be at once relieved by one of the other million.

In a very long mark one nearly always finds the bird, when one does find it, or when one's dog does, some yards nearer than where one thought it would be; but with these tall rushes one naturally takes one's mark by their conspicuous heads; but those heads are some way over the water, so that though the snipe appears to have fallen right on one par-

ticular rush, and though one keeps one's eye on it
while one walks ninety yards, it is actually to be
found at that spot on the surface of the water which
was eclipsed by the head of the rush from where
one stood when one fired the shot, that is to say a
good ten yards further on. One of my snipe took
a few minutes to find, for this reason; but the line
was all right, and so long as that is not many inches
out one finds one's snipe in the end. This is about
the most important part of shooting, for if one
could not find one's birds it would be much worse
than useless to kill them.

A duck or two got up, but far out of shot. It was
one of those bogs in which the aim of keeping one's
knees dry cannot quite be fulfilled, and it is in several ways difficult to walk; and yet it is not only
getting out of it that is satisfying, but I always look
back on it after with so much satisfaction that I
think there must be something in a large bog that
is more essentially Irish than in any other area of
land. Perhaps it is of all things the most obviously
and tangibly different from pavement, and perhaps
we weary of pavements more than we ourselves
suppose. As we reached the car another storm of
snow came at us from over the bog, but we pulled
up the windows against it and they were soon
white. And now night has come, and the wind is
blowing with changeable moods and there is certainly a great deal to be said for a bright fire.

On Sunday, partly because one is always in to
lunch, one is more likely to see a few friends and
neighbors than on another day: they also have
more leisure on that day. So one discusses the
state of Europe and whether the woodcock are in,
and what's going to happen next and what coverts
are holding foxes. To look at the world thus is
better than reading of it; better, too, than looking
at it fixedly out of one window; for it is better to
share with others one's ignorance of what machinery is going to do to our civilization, than to pry
alone into the dark of the future.

We have hot water laid on to this island from the
Gulf of Mexico, and whenever the wind is from
the southwest, as it nearly always is, we have
warmth from our central heating, while on the
same latitude further east they have almost Arctic
winters. But at any time that the wind changes
during the winter, even to go to the south, we
get the northern weather. It is blowing from the
south today and, though there is no snow, there
is that bleak cold in the air that makes men draw
nearer the firesides and woodcock go into the
woods. So I went to the woods with a few beaters,
to see if the woodcock were in; and I shot a few
of them and a few pheasants and a couple of rabbits. And then the south wind filled itself with
rain, and the afternoon set in all gray with mist,
and there would be a drip from the trees and the

beaters would all have got wet, and so I shot no
more. I may say that the number of pheasants one
shoots depends obviously on the number of eggs
that one has laid down. But sport is an ancient
thing, and I do not like to see it separated from any
of its ancient companions, the great winds and the
moon and the snow. Such things as these bring
the woodcock, so that he seems to come with some
of their splendor about him; but there is no such
splendor about the poulterer or the train that
delivers his goods. And apart from the feelings
with which one waits for the woodcock, and
watches the storms and the moon, on which his
arrival depends, there is the fact well known to all
who know the ways of the woods, that when they
are full of pheasants the woodcock will not come.
And so for twenty-five years I have laid down no
pheasants' eggs, and the ones we have are removed
from the poulterer's shop by at any rate as many
generations as separate ourselves from days almost
legendary.

Next day being a holy day, the snipe bogs no
longer had the lonely appearance that is natural to
those waste places. Here and there one would
hear from the fields the cries of young men playing
hurley, but many of these young men and many
boys were to be seen walking in small bands past
patches of furze, or among the brambles of derelict
woods from which most of the timber was gone,

and along the edges of bogs and such wild places, accompanied, of course, by the friend of man; all of them, dogs and men, inspired with the same hope, which was that the dog might catch a rabbit. And beyond the hope, no doubt, lay a day-dream that they might even chance on a hare. And with this hope and this day-dream dancing before them I met boys wherever I went. Even if the boys were not in clear view, there were always eyes watching from behind patches of furze, behind trees, or over the tops of hedges.

Even where snipe were not disturbed it made shooting a difficult and uneasy pastime, and I did not get many snipe until I came to the river, whose banks are strictly preserved for the sake of the coursing, and whose kind owners allow me to shoot the snipe. There there were no bands of young sportsmen and I got a few more snipe. When I got back to the road the golden plover were in the sky high up and shaped like big Vs, as though traveling on a long journey; but they were not traveling, for one saw if one watched them long enough that they had no particular course and were almost circling. Before nightfall they would be down to the fields over which they were now sailing. Near a house at the roadside I met a boy of seven or eight, who like myself was out with a weapon. His was a catapult, wrought I should say from the inner tube of a motor tire. I do not know what he hunted, perhaps he waited for a sparrow, or he may have put his hopes on the million-to-one chance of a lion coming that way, or, for that matter, a unicorn. But at any rate he had his catapult and was ready, and would have shown little mercy to sparrow, lion or unicorn, had any of them passed by on that holiday.

Suddenly the golden plover began to dip, and came down steeply beyond some haystacks. I had met them earlier in the day and got one, but at the haystacks my maneuver failed, and they all got safely away. And then I remembered a field where I had lain out for them in other years, a field over which they used to flight at evening. They might do so still, and I should not know if I merely wondered about it and went home to my tea. So as evening was coming on we motored to the gate in the field, and took a rug from the motor and carried it to the part of the field over which I had remembered them flighting, and lay down on it wearing a thick coat which was light in color and would not show up against the grass. The west was cloudy, with golden chasms amongst the rock-like clouds. Very soon the stillness was broken by the notes of the golden plover and the faint whirr of their wings, going over high. But it was a long time before they dipped at all, and when they did they flew over another field, and I just heard them in the distance and went to it. And one small

bunch of them came by me, and I got one. A few
fields away, as I came back in the dark, the lights
of a town were shining here and there, intensely
bright in comparison to any light still lingering
over the sunset. There was a certain beauty in
them at that hour, when nothing else had color.
I suppose that for animals roaming the fields by
night these lights have as much mystery as have
the stars for us.

And probably this mystery never diminishes, as
the mystery of the stars diminishes for us under the
prying of our large telescopes. But in the case of
these brighter lights there is a menace added to
mystery, and they are avoided like curses, except
by the fox, whose cunning teaches him to overcome
the terror that there is in the lights of man, in
order to snatch his food, which he knows is to be
found clucking about the houses of men. Notes of
stray golden plover calling for their companions
rang now quite near me, but it was too dark to
shoot. With my small bag I turned homeward,
thinking of warmth and tea, and thinking, too, of
an old cottage that I had passed earlier in the day,
a thatched cottage by the road, at a point at which
I often left the car, to walk to some rushy fields in
which I used to find snipe. I used to see a woman
standing in her doorway as I went by, and her dog
used always to be barking. But now one could see
at a glance, as one passed the cottage, that it was

desolate and given over to weeds. I cannot recollect exactly by what one saw this; it was not only that there was no smoke going up from the chimney; it must have been by a certain look in the weeds, a certain air of ownership. I said to my gamekeeper: "Why! You remember that cottage. It's all in ruin now."

And he said, "There was only an old woman living there, and I'd say that when she died it would go along with her."

XIX

Weeds and Moss

ON the night that followed the holy day it froze, and the morning was dank and cold again. It is as though winter is muttering threats, but has sent no storms as yet. As a very small frost is sufficient to banish the snipe from their feeding-grounds, my keeper collected some beaters and we went to another wood. But the cold had not been enough to put the woodcock in; or else it was that because this wood has been thinned during summer and autumn, the few home-bred woodcock whose resort it is had left it, and the rumor had got about amongst wild things that live in woods that there was something wrong about this wood. Or else the woodcock newly arrived, that came by the moon of November, and had known the wood last year, found all the furniture altered, and did not like the changes that had been made, but, finding some tree-trunk gone, which had always been a protection against the north wind, were ill content with the wood and went elsewhere. Whatever the cause, I shot pigeons and rabbits but saw never a single woodcock. There are some to whom the rabbits will be welcome, so the morning was not wasted.

In the afternoon the fog came crawling in, narrow-
ing the view slowly, so that I was reduced to this
poor expedient of writing about shooting, instead
of doing it. And now the fog is gone, but the
stars are cold and bright as though the winter had
not quite made up its mind.

And now while winter hovers let me turn for a
moment to trifles, in fact to boots. One walks many
miles with boots when one is shooting, and my
remarks on this trivial matter may save some
sportsman an uncomfortable walk. And this is my
advice about shooting-boots; to order where one
can give orders, and to request elsewhere, that one's
wet shooting-boots should never be put in any room
where there is a fire. For, if they are, the odds are
scarcely a hundred to one against somebody putting them near enough to the fire to fry them, which
means that the boots will not last a hundred days
of wear before some part of them hardens to about
the toughness of wood; and, as fried leather cannot be softened, it would be cheaper to buy a
wooden pair to start with.

Another thing that I have to say about boots
applies chiefly to boots in Ireland where the snipe-
bogs mostly are. I have heard shooting men more
than once or twice say that they have holes bored
in the soles of their boots to let the water out. This
is a heresy; for water in winter can be cold enough
actually to hurt one's feet, but it very soon warms

Philip D. Gendreau, New York

RUINS OF MUCKROSS ABBEY, NEAR KILLARNEY

Philip D. Gendreau, New York

PASSING ONE OF THE BEAUTIFUL LAKES OF KILLARNEY

when it has been in one's boots awhile; but, if one has holes in them, one insures a continuous supply of perfectly cold water. Once I bought a pair of waders up to my thighs, and they were made several inches higher on one side than on the other, adding to their weight without increasing their usefulness. This shows what funny things people will sometimes do in shops, for they might have noted in the nearest pond that by the time the water came over any side of the boot it would flood the whole boot. Such boots are deceptive, and may lead the wearer to think that he has more to spare than he actually has.

Our southwest wind has whimsically returned, and we set off in search of golden plover, which seem to be in the country as they were four years ago, and as they have scarcely been since. I do not know on what winds they ride, nor what storms turn them back: if I did, I should learn from them as much about that depression near Iceland as we hear from the B.B.C. But, wonderful as wireless is, and learned as are our scientists, I feel that the birds know all the news of the weather forecast, and some of it they unwittingly tell us, writing the news with long Vs in the sky and bringing inland the tale of storms upon northern seas.

The outwitting of golden plover depends, in one of its branches, on going to the right spot in a hedge, while another man goes round to the far

side of a field and drives them over. But I did not
go to the right spot in the hedge, and only got one.
Then I drew a small snipe-bog blank, because it
had been drained. But my gamekeeper pointed
out that there was no harm in that, for it would be
just the same again in two or three years. And this
is undoubtedly true, for soil and air in Ireland
seem to be at one in bringing back the bog to its
own, wherever man has lifted the spade against it.
The soil seems to work for the bog, while the damp
air fights against man. And so the spade is laid by,
and the bog steals softly back; and in a few years
there it is again, as though man had never troubled
its ancient stillness. All over the world the struggle
between civilized man and untamed earth is the
primary human interest. Tolstoy says that when
men speak of agriculture they discuss only the nature of the soil and overlook the nature of the man
that has to till it, which, as he rightly says, is of
equal importance. And both these natures are
made by the wind and the weather.

Memorials to this struggle may be found all over
Ireland, and they mostly seem memorials to the
victors, the wind and the weather. Sometimes one
sees a little square of low green mounds in a field,
that were once the walls of a cottage, sometimes
the bare towers of a castle, or towers that seem to
keep themselves warm by clutching a cloak of ivy;
for castles and cottages have been equally over-

thrown by the will of the southwest wind, with its listlessness that seems to defeat enduring purpose and its damp that overthrows mortar. Where cottages are attacked those two forces seem to be equally triumphant, the mud walls falling down and none caring to build them up; but in the case of the castles their magnificent masonry is still standing against the damp, and yet they have surrendered to weeds and moss and jackdaws, till one wonders if there is anything in Ireland that will hold out long against these.

Between the castle and the graveyard of Trimlestown I saw the golden plover in large flocks today, going up and down over a field in the distance and alighting just out of sight. We planned where I should go, and I asked my keeper to drive the golden plover to me, which he agreed to do, though remarking that it is harder to drive golden plover right than to maneuver an army. He maneuvered them quite well; and it is no use wishing now that I had gone to the best place, where I would have been close to a huge flock; but I got four of them. Then to two small snipe-bogs, one of them blank, and the other only providing two snipe; and so home. These are days when a dark shadow hung over Ireland, and over the Empire; today indeed is December 10th, 1936; but I have undertaken to write this book, and so must get on with it whether history frowns or smiles.

The next day has come, and it is raining hard. It is curious how one's mind welcomes a rainy day; not openly, yet pry into its recesses and it does welcome it sometimes. For a rainy day keeps one indoors. Apply too much logic to this and it would appear that one could stay indoors any day, whether it rained or not. But logic, like whisky, loses its beneficial effect when taken in too large quantities. I mean that to throw off a glass of whisky neat, merely because it happens to be standing handy, is not necessarily good; and in the same way a thing may be logically true and yet it may not be always good to apply it there and then. For supposing I stayed indoors, not lured out by sport, or supposing any man stayed indoors without powerful reason, not being taken into the open air by whatever usually takes him out, as sport takes me, it would constitute a triumph of indolence over sport, or over the other man's occupation, whatever it be, and it would be a triumph that indolence would not soon forget, and indolence would establish itself firmly.

Indolence has other antagonists besides sport, but sport is one of them, and however idle some may suppose sportsmen to be, we are at least sharpening our wits against the west wind or the north wind, whereas there is nothing to put any edge on them as we sit before the fire. It is a terrible thing to take exercise as one sometimes takes it in a ship, walking eight times round the deck; for one's thoughts are always then turned inwards upon one's liver, wondering when one will have walked enough for it. But the sportsman's thoughts are turned outwards away from his lights and liver, which thrive none the worse for that; and so his thoughts are free to mingle with their betters, the four winds and the snow. And the more I think of the strong winds that blow in a sportsman's face, the pleasanter they seem to be, because I am not out in them, but am sitting before a fire; and the gray shapes of the rain go by like the ghosts of giants.

In the afternoon the rain lifted a little and I went to a small and neighboring bog. There was only one snipe on it and I got him, though it took me two shots to do it. Had there been more, I should probably have missed most of them, for over all that low land the darkness made by the rain hung like a dome.

Night came, and we heard the farewell of the King.

XX

The Wind and the Wet Against the Cottages

I SAW today one of the very things I was writing about in the last chapter. I went after snipe after a night of rain, which had had the effect of moving them from the bogs in which I expected to find them. But, coming down the side of a green hill to one of these bogs, I came on four green lines that marked the site of a cottage. One could still see where the door had stood, and another line showed in the center, where an inner wall had divided the cottage into two rooms. None of these mounds was more than a foot high, and all were overgrown with grass, and nothing else remained to show that a cottage had been there; nothing else but these five low mounds and my memory; for I remember, and it does not seem so many years ago, that a herdsman used to live in a cottage that stood there, and he always used to come out of his house to meet me, when I came to shoot the bog. In my own lifetime the wind and the weather and the weeds have clutched this house and dragged it down to the earth, so that little more of it remains than what archeologists find when they search for buried cities. One does not fully understand Ireland if one overlooks the pace with which ruin floats on the gentle wind, and the grudge that the Irish soil seems to bear to civilization. Earth seems to triumph in the end over civilization everywhere, but a few decades in Ireland seem to have powers to bring down oblivion, such as only comes with a thousand years to Egypt.

The first bog was quite blank, and on the next one I only got two snipe. A path lies across this bog near to one end of it, probably made first by cut gorse-bushes or any timber that was handy, and then stones were laid down on that. I have never seen anyone crossing it, though probably a good many men do; the only creatures I have ever met on it are goats. By this path I always come out of the bog when I have finished shooting it, and where I come out of it there is an old cottage, standing in a little space fenced by whatever may have come handy during the last fifty years or so, such as bits of boxes, sticks, old broom-handles, and the end of a broken bedstead, all thrown together on scraps of wire. And the bog seems to watch the house as a panther watches an Indian village; sometimes it rises and goes through the little garden right up to the door, and in bad winters it goes stealing into the house itself: one day it will sweep the house altogether away, and a few years after only low mounds will show that men dwelt there at the edge of the bog for ages. I was invited to look inside

it only a week ago, and I got the impression in the
dimness beside the huge old fireplace that the thick
mud walls were very near to their end, and that
soon there would come a night when the bog below
and the storm above would join forces, and victory
would be with the weeds and the moss and the
water over this little outpost of man.

Of course when that happens the present occu-
pants will go to a modern laborer's cottage, in
which they will find dryness and shelter from
draughts, and brighter rooms; and oh, how they
will regret the huge, thick walls, crumbling and
damp though they were, and the great fireplace, in
spite of the winds that roared down the chimney,
and that dimness in all the corners, in which there
was room for dreams. And how they will miss the
storms coming over the bog by night to rattle their
door, and the sound of the sighing of reeds, and a
hundred other perfectly useless things! And how
I shall sympathize with them in their folly!

Why do people ever feel like that at all? Why
object to a laborer's cottage merely because millions are like it, or why care for crumbling walls
under a weedy thatch? I think it is because in our
hearts we like things to have meanings, and to tell
us at a glance what need of ours they fulfil and
what they are helping us to do. These cottages rose
from maternal Irish soil to shelter Irish people,
and their thatches are darkened by rain that the

southwest wind has led over them through the ages. They are a part of the countryside, and they clasp their people to it. But there are cottages being built now, in Ireland as elsewhere, that seem to mean so little that they could not tell to a traveler even what country he was in: doubtless such cottages are arising all over Europe, and no one could tell by the look of them whether he had crossed any frontier or not. Their physical advantages are so obvious that I need not write them down, whereas the spiritual advantage of the old cottages that link country and countryman are amongst those rare influences that, vital though they be and not imperceptible to any of us, are too delicate to define and to prove. But do not let it be thought that all the physical advantages are with the Ruritanian cottages, as we may call the cottages that represent the architecture of no particular country; I doubt if they will stand half as long as the old Irish cottages, and I am sure their thin brick walls are not so warm, and that the quiet of the old deep thatches will be strange to them.

A certain dissatisfaction with modern cottages is even expressed in a letter to the Westmeath Board of Health, which I have just seen quoted in the *Irish Times:*

"I want you to take my cottage to another side of the land. Where it is, is on a pass. The good people are displeased, and the life is frightened out of Minnie, for when she goes to the well for water she sees a little red man with a green cap and he laughs and jeers at her. He is one of the King fairies from Rawmore. They kick football in the race park, and my house is on the pass. I had to leave a drop of whisky on the window on Christmas night to keep them in good form. The house is haunted, and so is the plantation at the back. It is a terrible thing to make a man live in such a place in a Christian country. I am kept awake at night when there is a big match, and when I'm late for work Mr. Dick is vexed. The fairies in this place are no joke, and there are big ones in the race park. If I had a fairy man to go to like Conor Sheridan I used to hear my father talking about I would be all right, but I have not, and I want to tell you there's a leprechaun captain at Cummerstown."

This, I think, shows that not all modern cottages are entirely suited to the needs of the country.

The Westmeath Board of Health have decided that the Engineer should report on it.

I knew an old woman once who lived in a cottage beyond one of my woods. At one end of the cottage she had a cavernous fireplace, and gradually she stacked round it as much timber as she was able to collect from my wood in a long lifetime, except such as burned away in the fireplace to fill her dark room with warmth, a fireplace more suitable in

size to the hall of a feudal castle than to this small
building of mud. Weeds had so long obscured the
outside of her window and the huge mass of timber
so darkened everything inside, that even by day
there was little light in the cottage except for the
glow of the fire. To the far end from the fire it
was too dark to see; dim heaps of things seemed to
be moldering there, but I never knew what they
were. Though her door was all soft with decay,
it was still a door to her, and she asked me to give
her a lock for it. One day from a system of which
she knew nothing, with a tyranny that seemed to
bewilder her, there came talk of sanitary inspectors; and she implored me to save from these tyran-
nous people the cottage in which she had lived for
eighty years. Coming in on the wrong side, I
was able to do this for her; and she lived there
happily until one day her cottage fell, and she went
to live with relations, but her dog ran away and
was never heard of again. In a world of change
and struggle that cottage must have been to the dog
the one calm and abiding thing, situated exactly
at the center of the universe. And then one day it
fell, and he fled, probably fearing, poor thing, that
if he stayed near that field any longer the Milky
Way would come down on him next.

The next day was Sunday, and we went to lunch
with neighbors, and exchanged with them views
of this troubled world. The word neighbor was,

I may say, always a more elastic word in Ireland
than on the other side of the Channel, even before
the days of motors and before house-burning became a political issue. We went so far to see these
neighbors that we came to the rim of the view on
which Tara gazes. We came to hills on whose
summits one sees ancient stones, showing that the
huge view northwards to the small lakes and southwards over Meath, which can impress men of
today, must have awed the people of an earlier age,
till they expressed their awe by raising these stones
with their quaint carvings, which to them must
have expressed what they would say, but whose
message is dumb to us. Or it may be that what
impressed the Milesians, who buried their kings on
these hills, was less the great view from these hills
than the appearance of them in the distance, from
where they met on festival days at Tara. For the
hills of Slieve-na-Calliagh seem very blue from
Tara, and unlike the fields of this world; and the
long row of them going over the utmost rim of the
view might upon many an evening have hinted to
the people gazing from Tara that amongst that
gathering of dim blue mountains there was the
magic for which their hearts were yearning, and
of which their druids spoke. And so, when the end
came to the days of their kings, they carried them
there to the hills that seemed so mysterious, trust-
ing those far blue slopes to hold the mystery of

death. There the Milesians buried Ollamh Fodhla,
one of the chief of their kings, at the top of the
hill, with counties spread out all round him. I do
not know what hopes they had of heaven, but they
must have had a great love of earth who chose this
view.

The view today was almost veiled with rain. On
the way back I took one more look at it, from a hill
upon which a tower stands overlooking Kells and
from which one can see so much of the country that
I make an attempt to describe; but, although the
light of the afternoon should not yet have faded,
there was not much of it left beneath the tumultu-
ous clouds that were blowing by low before a powerful wind, and the hills of Meath seemed to be
of a blue verging on blackness, and only the somber
wood on the Hill of Fahan appeared clear to be
seen. When we came to Navan, lights were already
lit.

And today I set out to pay in part what I feel
to be a neglected debt, for I am to broadcast from
Dublin about the work of Francis Ledwidge.
Whether anyone will heed me I do not know, but
at least words of Ledwidge's will be heard by
many thousands, and that may in itself be some
slight fulfilment of a young poet's hopes. But
whether I speak his lines or not, I feel that they
are sufficiently lovely to take care of themselves
in the end. Posterity will still be there while this

planet keeps on her course, and if there be merit in Ledwidge's lines, as I believe there is, Posterity will have time to assess it.

And when I went to Dublin I found that Ireland had altered much overnight; for in the country one sees, far quicker than ever one does in a town, whatever changes are brought by the varying moods of the weather; and today I saw a snipe get up in a green field and fly over the road, and later I saw a stream that had also strayed from its haunts, and was suddenly wild and free, for it had been raining all night. The stream was all over the fields on our right for a mile; then it crossed the road, luckily underneath it, and went over the fields on our left. When streams do not keep to their banks it is hard to find snipe in the bogs, and I do not know where I shall look for any tomorrow.

On arriving at Dublin I went to the Kildare Street Club, which is to Ireland something more than what the Carlton Club is to England. There I saw the old faces I used to know, but only painted on canvas; for the club in recent years acquired portraits of several of its prominent members, and these are the faces that I used to know, whereas to many of the present members I notice that my own face is strange. Thence I went to jog the memory of Ireland, lest she quite forget Ledwidge.

A night of rain, and then frost, went by, and

the snipe will be frozen out of their bogs and the
rain will have kept the woodcock out of the woods,
for they hate the drip from the trees, so we went
after golden plover. And the frost was not hard
enough to send the golden plover away to the sea,
for it takes a bone in the ground to do that, and we
found them in the fields, feeding. We had several
maneuvers, each producing something; but perfect
success with golden plover is a thing that chance
and caution only bring to one after many efforts.
On this occasion I got no more than four, and a
snipe by the side of a stream. There is an important difference between dead thistles and dead
golden plover, which is that you cannot cook the
one and you can cook the other; and very good he
is when he is cooked. But, in spite of this difference, dead thistles and live golden plover are very
much alike in a field and either can be mistaken for
the other. We were discussing this very point, my
keeper and I, of a thick brown bunch in the field.
He said they were thistles. And as we discussed
them they flew.

And now a great wind outside is emphasizing
the advantages of a good fire.

XXI

Only About the Weather

ANOTHER day has come raging in, with a great
voice in the sky, the voice of the south wind, chasing clouds before it. And we went to a snipe-bog
which had, in some profusion, a feature that I have
neglected as yet to mention as an important part of
a snipe-shooter's country, that is to say streams and
ditches. It is a bog some way off, and to the south
of here, from which we can see the Dublin Mountains smiling back at the sun. We had not gone
there for two or three years, and my gamekeeper
gave me several reasons to account for the width
of the ditches; careful draining was one of these
reasons, and the floods that the recent rains have
brought was another. But the fact is that my gamekeeper is the same age as myself; and, though we
jumped all the ditches and streams, we found them
wide, and it is the years that have widened them.
I may say that when a ditch is wide enough for it
to be necessary to discard all weight that can be
discarded, there is no difficulty at all in throwing
a gun across from one man to another; and one
cannot fail to catch it, provided that it is thrown
horizontally.

A night of rain always leaves the snipe alert and
uneasy, and floods drive them to little high points
of the grassy islands, so that they see further; and
the two things together made them very wild. A
wind was raging, with rain in it, which made shooting harder still, and I only got two snipe, though I
happened to come on some pigeons on the way
back and got four of them; golden plover we met
with also, and my keeper went off to drive them;
but I have already recorded his view that it is
easier to maneuver an army, and on this occasion
the army just outmaneuvered their general. He
has, however, uttered the threat that we shall yet
get in with them, to such an extent that there will
be no room to close the door of the larder. Tonight there dines with us Dr. Gogarty, the famous
Irish wit. I do not think I shall be able to record
anything that he says, as I think it will be too indiscreet. My reason for this opinion is that rumor
has told me he has been having some trouble with
his publisher over parts of his new book, and he
himself has told me that the B.B.C. have been ob-
jecting to all the wittiest bits of a broadcast that
he is to give from Belfast. Thwarted therefore in
two directions with repression of all indiscretion,
his conversation, if there is anything in what psy-
chologists teach, is likely to be indiscreet.

There arrived while I was out a load of turf, as
we always call peat in Ireland. We live on that

fringe of green grazed by fat cattle, which lies
beyond the red bogs, and we are about ten miles
from the nearest. It is from the red bogs that they
quarry with spear-like spades the turf for the Irish
hearths. The scent of turf from a cottage round
here is a thing that one notices: further west they
would all be burning it. That scent in the air is,
of all odors, the most essentially Irish. Would
that this book could give to any reader the atmosphere of Ireland, as the smoke of turf can call it
up for me. In this smoke the spirit of Ireland
seems to lurk and hide. And here is an idea that
I will present to the manager of any theater who
desires to get an Irish atmosphere for some Irish
play: let him, if he can imitate it, have the sound
of a curlew calling occasionally in the distance and
let him send into the auditorium a whiff from a
smoldering sod of Irish turf; and he will get the
Irish atmosphere by those means, certainly more
cheaply, and perhaps more surely, than he has ever
got it before. Feeling that way about it, I sent for
a load of turf, though it is not the natural fuel of
this end of the island. And it arrived today. It
came from a bog whose name is an example of the
beauty there is so often in Irish names. The name
of the bog is Coolronan: through it runs the boundary between Meath and Westmeath, and the view
over it in at least one direction has that quality that
is so valuable in a view, which is that it is illimit-

able. In one direction it shares with desert and ocean the splendor of being unbounded by anything but the sky. And now the turf is glowing at me, with that glow of its own that never turns to flame, or only to faintest flame. But, mix the turf with wood, and you have all the merriment of flame combined with the turf's deep glow.

Last night a new moon was reported to me as having been observed, and being very wicked looking; but I think she must be a few days old, for my gamekeeper tells me that Old Moore has foretold a full moon for next Monday week, and now it is Thursday. As for her being wicked looking, I do not wonder, for there is a raging sky today and, looking at it beyond the fields while I was searching for golden plover, I saw the low sky light in the north; above that a bank of clouds lowered deep blue, with whitish-gray clouds racing across the darkness; above them the sky, at half past two, was nearly as black as night, with more white clouds racing over it, wildly away from the west. It might well be what my gamekeeper estimated it, the wickedest-looking sky he had ever seen. Such weather has scattered the snipe away from the bogs; and has driven the ducks from the pond that they flight to, for when floods are out they are off to look for the earthworms. And so we went to find the golden plover. I got four of them and

came home early, but even earlier the light was
fading.

On the next day we went to a bog to look for
snipe. All the ditches were full to the brim, and
most of the bog was flooded. When the soft banks
of streams or ditches that run through bogs are full
to the top they make very difficult jumping. A
herdsman on our way to the bog told us it was full
of snipe, but such information is not always welcome, for snipe are never seen unless they are flying, so that any news of them means they have been
disturbed. A wind was still raging. We found
some snipe that had not been flooded out, and I shot
four. But in the opinion of my gamekeeper, who
has considerable experience, they were wild as the
Devil's father. So we left that bog and went to a
much smaller one, no more than a marshy corner
of a field, where I got three in half a minute. I
must write no more of the weather, for it is everywhere considered the dullest of topics, and is of
little interest to people in towns, which is, after
all, where most men live. And yet in the open
country the weather is a beautiful thing, and is
constantly changing and is of the greatest importance to all whose living is made in the fields. And
there it is in the sky, to be seen by everybody, like
a series of vast pictures, replaced every few minutes; and beyond the visible scene are the omens

and portents, foretelling storms or sunshine or snow.

By the brightness of the sword of Orion, by the flight of a flock of geese, or by the reddening of berries, these things may be reckoned, so that one concerned with that humble topic, the weather, has interests neither narrow nor far aloof from our lot; they embrace fields and hedge-rows, and one of their boundaries is the Milky Way. If a society for the enjoyment of conversation were formed, and the only topic allowed when its members met were the weather, it might be full of descriptions of lovely scenes, and as varied as any topic could be, at any rate in Ireland, and it might be full of wise forebodings, and of some practical value. Only, at the meetings of such a society the weather reports of the wireless would have to be barred, for their is a certainty in such scientific pronouncements that would bludgeon speculation and drive all fancies away. And, by the way, some society of this sort is surely needed, if only to rescue thousands from the comparative monotony of bridge; for there is not the variety in the thirteen cards of hearts, diamonds, clubs or spades that there is in the winds that come from the four quarters.

As for the gambling interest, money could just as well be staked on the morrow's weather; and there again the wireless would have to be barred, and resort to it would be cheating. Think of the strength of the hand of a man who had seen thirty geese flying inland, against a man who was fore-telling mild weather upon some much weaker suit. Did I say that I would write no more of the weather? I am not sure that it is possible to write of Ireland and to fulfil this promise: all countries and all peoples are made what they are by the weather, but in Ireland you almost see these things in the making, so strong is the southwest wind, so full of damp, so indolent its mood, and so much its strength seems to be used to impose its moods upon earth and buildings and men.

Thousands of suns have shone upon millions of buds of heather, thousands of winds have beaten the blossoms down, and long gray rains have patted them into place; and so were made the Irish bogs, and the peat that we call turf. And I sit now by a fire of the turf that was made by ages of weather, and care no more for any weather outside.

XXII

A Great Hunt

DAY came in with cold, with a wind from the
south, but the frost of the night was soon gone and
had not been hard enough to freeze out snipe. So
I went to some small marshes and marshy fields.
One of them lay under a steep mound-like hill with
gorse on the top, as there nearly always is on such
hills, and the marsh ran right to the walls of a
farmhouse, where the snipe lay very close, being
accustomed to men's coming and going; but they
were difficult to shoot when they got up, because,
on account of the direction of the wind, I was walking straight to the house and had to see the snipe
well clear of it before I fired. Another lay along
a railway embankment, as small marshes often do,
the water coming in where the earth has been taken
out for the railway.

The farmhouse here had one of the most domes-
tic and homely haystacks I have ever seen, for it
abounded with little niches that were the warm
homes of hens and dogs and cats. There is a tendency nowadays in Ireland to turn bohereens into
roads, and this tendency enabled me to get with my
car closer to the next small marshy patch than I

had ever been able to do before. And a fourth
marsh we drove, that is to say my keeper went
round it, and put some of the snipe over me;
though, the wind not being exactly right, only two
came within shot. I very rarely drive snipe, but
we did so here because there is a house that would
be right ahead of me, and within shot, if I walked
them up. I have perhaps said enough about snipe,
even though, after the phoenix, the snipe is, of all
feathered things, probably the most Irish bird. But
one thing more I will say of snipe, before I leave
them, for it deals with the important matter of
picking them up, and is a thing that I have not yet
mentioned, that is to say that when two snipe are
down, and the sportsman picks up one, he must
make quite sure that it is the one he thinks it is;
otherwise he will be looking for the second snipe
in the wrong place. That happened today while
the snipe were being driven; for I had two down,
one in a cabbage-garden beside a cottage and the
other forty or fifty yards from it in a field. Searching round the cottage we disturbed a cat just at the
right moment, and found the snipe with only its
head eaten off; then we looked for the other one
in the field.

But we had underrated the observation of the
cat, which had seen the snipe drop in the field; and
that was the one it had retrieved for itself.

After ten minutes' searching in the field, we

looked in the cabbage-garden as a last resort, and
soon found the other snipe. I got eleven snipe and
a rabbit, in all; and perhaps that is enough about
snipe.

I should be leaving a staring gap in my life, or
in the life of any surviving Irish landlord, were I
to say nothing of hound-puppies. I was reminded
of them today, as I passed near the stables on my
way out to shoot, and there I saw a hound-puppy
on a lawn quietly eating a boot. Hound-puppies
are sent out in pairs to houses throughout the
county in the summer and are brought up on a diet
of boots and rags, varied by an occasional hat, and
find their own sport, chasing whatever will run in
coverts near to the house. By the end of March,
just when one is getting to know them rather well,
they are called for and taken away from their life
of indiscipline, to be members of a pack, and to
learn no more to look at a rabbit than a soldier
would play on parade with some toy of his infancy.
I have only one hound-puppy here now; the other
died in a plague of hysteria that swept the county.
We had better find out, and find out quickly, what
change it is in our own ways that has brought this
disease upon dogs. For dogs do not change their
ways; it is we that are doing the changing. And
we have done something that not even dogs can
stand. And they are usually tougher than we. If it
is bad food, the same commercial system that sup-

plies it is likely to poison us too. If it is something else, we had better find it out quickly; for it must be something pretty unwholesome, whatever it is. But above all things let us bear in mind that it is something quite new, and that some change must have brought it, and that it is we who change and not animals.

Before light faded today I saw what I have sometimes heard of, but rarely seen, a parliament of the rooks. They came down about a hundred and fifty yards from our windows, and blackened the grass. There were far more of them than could have possibly come for feeding; there were more of them to the acre than there could have been worms for them. Sometimes they rose in a black wave and lighted again, or blew about in the south-west wind like black leaves and returned again to the place from which they had risen. They were not there long, and I do not know why they came, but it was a great meeting; and I have the feeling that something of great importance was discussed there, but none of us will ever know what it was. So let us turn back to our own affairs, which to us are more easily understood, and to us seem more important. I was talking of a hound-puppy eating a boot. What memories he brings back! I hope to ride within a reasonable distance of him yet, but my best hunts are behind me, hunts that I saw

when I could ride thirteen stone, and bits of which
I remember, sitting before the fire.

And if I have said that turf gives scarcely any
flame, I should correct that now, for faint flames
go up from it like the ghosts of flames, all golden,
or like the spirits of flames in some fiery paradise
to which good flames go, very thin and calm and
restful. And when these flames sink they can be
stirred up again by hitting the sods with a poker,
which makes showers of golden sparks. And in
front of such a fire I am thinking of old hunts,
brought back to my memory by the puppy chewing
a boot. There was the time when I had come in
from a very good day with my harriers, for I had
a pack of my own in those days. It was a day in
March, and I was having a cup of tea, after three
good runs with my hounds: the first was twenty
minutes, my hunting diary tells me, the next twenty-
five and the last one thirty-five, and I felt I had
had a good day. It was almost five o'clock and
there was still plenty of light, when, looking out
of the window, I saw cattle running near a wood.
And it turned out that the Ward Hounds were in
the wood, and coming in my direction. I had a
fresh horse saddled and got on to him as soon as
I could, and galloped off to overtake the Ward. I
came up with them before I had gone two miles;
and there was I with a fresh horse, among men
who had already done three miles when they came

to my wood, and it was their second hunt that day.

It was a piece of luck such as might come one's way once in a lifetime; and here it had come to me. And when it came, it came abundantly. For not only was I there on a fresh horse with the Ward, but I was in one of the finest hunts they were ever to have. I do not say that they have not had many as good, but it was one of their great hunts and it was the first time that they had enlarged that wonderful hind that became an outlier, living mostly in my woods and being hunted off and on for several years, giving a memorable hunt every time. Of course with my fresh horse, once I had caught them up, I had the advantage that a man with a joker in his hand would have at a game of bridge, or a bowler at cricket enjoying the use of a Mills bomb. We were going westwards and a tired field were dropping away, until there was only one other man beside myself with the hounds, a Mr. Davis, as my hunting diary records. A house that I knew flashed by us, and I knew we had come eight miles from my own door, going straight. And then for a very brief time I remember being alone with the Ward Hounds, which I never had been before and was never to be again.

Brindley, the huntsman, soon came up again and one of the whips and, I think, Mr. Davis, although the *Irish Times* of March 15th, 1904, only records Brindley and one whip and me as reaching the end of the run. And the end of the run was simply the end of the day; with the Boyne before us and night coming up from behind, Brindley called his hounds off and we turned homewards. Then night came down in earnest and even the white patches on the hounds' backs disappeared, and the only light we saw was from sparks from the horses' hooves. It had been a run of two hours, the first twenty minutes of which I had not seen, and I had nothing to boast of in getting to the end of it, when luck played so large a part; but the time when I was alone with them in the sunlight, and Brindley in the twilight at the bank of the Boyne, and the dark road, riding home, live clearly yet in my memories.

XXIII

A Bad Night to be Out

A NOTHER Sunday came round, and we lunched
with neighbors. I wasted some of the time during
which I might have heard a good deal of news of
local interest, by trying to convince a neighbor at
table by argument. For there was a litter of pup-
pies in the house, and that gave rise to the topic
of mutilating their tails, and I tried to convince
my neighbor against this cruelty by which we gain
nothing and our good friends lose so much. But
people are cruel or kind by nature and not by logic,
and Fashion is more powerful than any argument
of mine, so that I failed utterly. And yet thirty
years ago I used to employ the same arguments in
the hunting-field, or rather on roads jogging from
covert to covert, against cutting the tails off horses;
and I failed just as completely then, and people
thought me just as mad for trying then for the sake
of horses as they think me now for my efforts to
spare dogs; and then one day most of the world
came my way, and hardly anybody cuts tails off
horses now.

And I write this to encourage all who attack
abuses; for the abuse looks firm as a mountain for

years, and then one day it collapses flabbily. The
mutilation of dogs will go the way of other wild
whims of fashion; but I don't know when. I will
not argue with my reader about it, or attempt to
instruct him in the uses dogs have for their tails,
for a little observation will reveal many of these
uses, while those that have not leisure for such
observation may credit the Creator with under-
standing His work. Some may think that I who
hunt foxes am not the right person to protest against
cruelty to animals. And that may be so. And yet,
better have the wrong· person protesting than nobody at all. And there is a glamor in the brush of
a fox that makes its pursuit a great temptation: I
only ask those who rob dogs of their tails to abstain
from this great deprivation where they have so
little temptation to do it; only a debased eye, which
will very soon right itself after they have seen a
few natural terriers.

Being mainly amongst racing men I learned a
use for a horse's tail that I had not thought of
before.

Next day I went to a snipe-bog on which I had
only got two snipe ten days ago, and this time I
got nine, and on a small bog a few fields away five
more. The uncertainties of sport depend on so
many things, that they must remain merely uncertain. But one reason why I got more snipe this
time was that three of my fourteen were jacks; and

when the jacks are there the foreign snipe are in, for the jack is migratory, and there are scarcely any of them in the country until the flight comes over the sea, and about half the full snipe that we . have in the bogs come with it. The next bog I went to was blank.

"Was anybody shooting it?" I asked of a couple of men who were looking on.

"Sure nobody shoots it only yourself," said one of them. "The snipe will be back tomorrow and you'll always find plenty of them here."

"The only thing I'd be afraid of," said the other man, "would be if anybody built an hotel, and advertised for people to come and get the shooting. They might come along in a motor car."

"Ah," said the first man, "the best thing if he did that would be to shoot him. Sure anybody would do that for you," he added, turning to me.

"I wouldn't say that would be a good plan," said the other man thoughtfully. "Sure he'd only have what they call executors. And the first thing they'd do would be to sell the hotel to somebody else. But it might be better to blow the hotel up one night. Sure a charge of dynamite would do it."

"Aye," said the first man, "that'd be best."

"Is there any hotel anywhere near?" I asked.

"Sure there is not," said the men.

"Then we needn't bother about the dynamite," I said.

"Begob, you're right," said the first man. "Sure you've thought it out well."

I have slightly altered the actual conversation, because to write and sell the exact words of a man gives me the feeling of having stolen them. The moralist would say that the thing is no better for being disguised. And of course he would be right.

The evening of another day has come, and I sit again in front of my fire of turf, the same kind of turf that I have been walking during the day, for I went to a red bog to look for woodcock. It was a mild day, when they are likely to be away from the woods and may be found in the heather. One walks down a lane to it from a corner of the demesne-wall of one of the finest houses in Meath. The wall leans outward in many places, ready to fall if the ivy should chance to leave go of it, and the house is a windowless ruin, burnt for political reasons, upon which I will not enlarge, for they are well enough known in Ireland, while my English readers are not likely to have that inner knowledge of politics which it is necessary to have before all the advantages of burning the house of a man with whose politics you are in disagreement are clearly understood.

It stands on a hill, this house, and the long row of its windows looking south over woods that are now in ruin, like so much else, must have seen so much sunshine in that wide view, all through the bright months, that perhaps whoever named it may have had the idea that Summer itself dwelt under the slopes of that hill. I have the kind permission of the owner of it to shoot the red bog that lies wild at the edges of the estate, and so I went down the bohereen that leads to the bog, past one or two cottages where surprised dogs barked, till I came to a small farmhouse with a lovely thatch, and after that nothing dwelt but wild things. I had brought a few beaters in another car, and we walked the bog for two and a half hours, but it had been burned less than three years ago and the heather was not quite enough to give the cover that woodcock prefer. However, I got four of them, and four snipe and a rabbit; and for a smaller bag than this I would have gone further for the pleasure of walking that strange wild land that goes by the name of the red bog. I noticed no turf-stacks on it this year for the first time, and when I came to a promontory about twelve feet high, and little more than twenty yards long and broad, I realized that the reason for the absence of turf-stacks was that, with the exception of this high bit, the entire bog had probably been cut away.

They could do it in a few centuries, and that is what must have happened. There is still bog below what has been cut, but it is probably too wet for men to work it. The only difference that the cutting has made, besides slightly lowering the level, is that there may be a little more moss and a little less heather, but the difference is barely perceptible. On two sides of it are pine woods, so that one usually knows in which direction a woodcock is going to fly. The flight of these birds is so rapid, that after shooting at them one finds it a little easier to kill snipe. As we had our lunch on the bog I noticed a very bright patch of sky, and the wind seemed to have shifted a little more to the west, and it looks as if we shall have cold weather. As we left the bog we put up a fox, and he went away to the dry land.

"The devil go along with him," said the farmer who lived by the edge of the bog. And probably the devil does, for he is against all our orderliness and our conventions, as the fox is against our chickens. They are two wild spirits. As a fox-hunter I rejoice in the fox. Do clergymen have the same feeling about the devil?

It is the day on which we have a Christmas tree for the school children here, and I arrived too late to see it, for children have to be home before dark; but I was in time to see them all before they left, making with varied instruments the kind of music that perhaps was made by the musicians of Nebuchadnezzar on the occasion when people were required to worship the image that he, Nebuchadnezzar the King, had set up. Thus Father Christmas is glorified. And now the turf from Coolronan is not only glowing, but is sending up its thin ghosts of golden flames; and, outside, the sky is luminous with moonlight, from a moon eight days old, but the stars are shining brightly out of the glow. It is cold and still, and the sound of water falling a long way off, where a stream goes over a weir, comes very clear through the stillness.

And that night brought the frost that all omens were prophesying, and I went to a wood with beaters, to look for woodcock. It is a square wood with a gorse in the middle of it, originally designed as a fox-covert; and foxes and woodcock seem to live there together quite happily. But it was not an enduring frost, and the drip, which these birds hate, had already begun; and we only saw two woodcock, which I was fortunately able to get, as well as some rabbits. It was not the weather in which to look for any more woodcock, and yet the frost was a little too hard for one to be sure of snipe on the bogs.

And all of a sudden I remembered the purpose of this book, which I have set aside so long. And that purpose is to lay before my readers what the people of Ireland really think about their new political system. It had almost slipped my memory, crowded out by things that to me are more interesting than politics. I shot no more that day, and decided to go and see Old Mickey as soon as possible; though, various trifles delaying me, I did not actually start till the following day. On that day I started off by car towards the blue west that one can see from Tara, and lunched by the roadside on sandwiches beyond Trim, and went on leisurely, watching the landscape growing wilder as we went west; and, it being Christmas Eve, the daylight began to fade before one had thought of evening, and was already fading when I arrived at Cranogue. And there was Old Mickey sitting in his doorway as usual.

"I came to ask you what you promised to tell me," I said to him.

"And what was that?" said Old Mickey.

"What the people think of this new government that we've got," I said.

"Aye; and, sure, I'll tell you," said Old Mickey.

"And what do they really think?" I asked.

"Would you ask that man to drive that yoke a little further away," said Old Mickey, pointing to my chauffeur. "For it's a very conspicuous object in front of my door and people will be gathering to look at it."

So I asked the driver to take the car into the yard at Sharkey's Hotel, which is at the other end of the street, and to wait for me there, where cars are not quite so rare as in front of Old Mickey's door.

When he was gone Old Mickey pulled out his pipe and crammed some tobacco in and was about to speak, when a young man came by from some work that he had been doing in the fields and went to his home further up the street. Old Mickey paused and watched him until he was out of hearing, and was, I think, about to speak again, when we saw another young man approaching us. I looked up the road to be sure that we should be disturbed no more when this man had gone by; but I saw that it would not be as I had hoped, for behind him, straggling along the road at various intervals, there were several more.

"Where are they all coming from?" I asked.

"Sure, they're coming from their work," said Old Mickey.

"But it's not yet four o'clock," I said.

"It is not," said Old Mickey.

"Why are they all coming home so early?" I asked.

"Begob," said Old Mickey, "you've chosen a queer day to be out at this hour so far from your home. I'll be going in myself in a few minutes, though I wouldn't mind sitting here for another hour at my own door. Aye, a man's all right at his own door, when he can slip into the house in a moment, and there he is in the lamplight in front of his fire, with the door shut and barred, and all hell might be loose outside; but you're a long way from your home. And yet in that motor car maybe

you'd be safe enough, for they'd never go near a
new-fangled thing like that."

"Who?" I asked.

"The dead," said Old Mickey.

"The dead?" I said.

"And who else?" said Old Mickey. "Who else
would be out on a Christmas Eve but the dead?
And you writing a book about Ireland, and you
don't know that."

I did know it as a matter of fact, but I had forgotten it. I remembered the days when Christmas
presents given to workmen on that day had to be
given early, so that they could get to their homes
by daylight, before the spirits of the departed
might be about.

"Sure, those lads have, none of them, motor cars.
And would they want to be coming home alone in
the dark with dead spirits nosing after them like
hounds, and maybe a rush being made at them as
they go by the graveyard? Begob, they might
never get to their homes at all."

"Do they believe all that still?" I asked Old
Mickey.

"They do not," said Old Mickey, "and more's
the pity. But they won't take the risk, for all that.
Times have changed a lot, and Ireland has am-
bassadors in all the countries of the world; but I
don't know who there is to protect a young lad

now, if the dead made a set at him, any more than there ever was."

But in a matter like this, where I wish to set plain facts before my reader, I thought it better to go to the fountainhead, and ask the young men themselves who were hurrying home, instead of offering Old Mickey's secondhand views about them.

"Good evening," I called to the first of them as he came by.

"Good evening," said he.

"You're coming home early from work, aren't you?" I asked.

"My mother's wetting the tea early today," he said, "and I'm coming home for my tea."

"Why is she making it so early?" I asked.

"Because she has a good fire going," he said, "and if she waited too long it might sink lower and not be able to boil the water."

"Ah, he's only talking," said Old Mickey.

But I determined to stick to firsthand evidence, and called out to the next one that went by, asking him the same question.

"Ah, sure, my work's all done," he said, "so I've nothing more to do, and I'm coming home."

And a third man came by and I asked him the same question.

"Ah, sure, I want to sell a dog to a man," he said,

"and if I wait any longer the man will be gone."
And he hurried on quickly.

And when he had gone I asked Old Mickey once
more the question whose answer I am so anxious to
place before my readers, and I believe that Old
Mickey was about to tell me, when yet another
returning laborer appeared. And then Old Mickey
rose.

"Begob," said he, "it would be a terrible night
to be out."

And he thanked me for the honor I had done
him, and went in and shut his door. I never knew
what fear drove Old Mickey indoors, whether the
fear of being overheard talking politics, or the
fear that certainly awed his generation, whatever
the young men felt, the fear of being overtaken in
the twilight on Christmas Eve by the dead.

XXIV

St. Stephen

So I walked from Old Mickey's house to Sharkey's Hotel to get my car; and there I saw Sharkey standing in his back doorway, that looked into the yard. We greeted each other. "Do you find people about here," I asked, "still having any superstition about Christmas Eve?"

"Ah, that's all nonsense," he said. "Sure, no one believes it."

"Could you tell me the way to the graveyard?" I asked. "I wanted to have a look at it."

"Over there," he said, pointing.

"The light's not very good," I said, "and I can't quite see. Would you mind coming with me to show me the way?"

"Begob," he said, "I would gladly, only I have a man in there that I must serve with a drink. He'll be bawling for me if I don't go at once. But I'd be glad to show you any other time."

And he went into Sharkey's Hotel, and I went to my car, and the driver turned up the lights and we started for home. As these words will not be in print before the spring, I have still ample time to get from Old Mickey, on some day when he will

have more leisure, the information that is essential
to this book. So for the present I put the matter
out of my mind, and came back by a road strangely
lonely, except for the occasional lights of motors
rising like sudden dawns, and disappearing as suddenly into the night. And sometimes we saw the
apple-green eyes of small animals surprised by the
glare of our lamps.

So we came home; and, at midnight, neighboring bells rang in Christmas. I do not write of
Christmas Day, for that is not Irish property, nor
even European, and we have Christmas cards even
from Mohammedans upon our mantelpiece here. I
will write of that if ever a publisher persuades me
to undertake a book to be called *My World*. When
our civilization perishes, will whoever take our
place remember Father Christmas? Or will some
heretical sect, with zealous ignorance, put Tom
Smith in his place? It may well be so, for the
fragments of palaces and the ruins of old traditions
are all strange to succeeding ages; so the mortal
Tom Smith may get mixed up during the next age
of barbarism with the immortal Father Christmas,
and even come out on the other side with a pur-
loined immortality. I am not presuming to at-
tribute to posterity any muddle such as we do not
ourselves often make about those who were mighty
in Egypt.

Christmas passed and then came St. Stephen's

Day, and I went to shoot a red bog, for the moon was nearly full, making the grass by night all white, from our windows. I came to the bog by a lane, that ran to a cottage and soon afterwards faded away. By the side of the lane was a stile, with steps leading up to it made by very large stones; but with this stile and the steps the work of man ended, but for a tiny field that had once been cut from the bog, as one could see from old scars in it; and above the field the bog lowered dark and untamed. Let me mention for the sake of those who may be unacquainted with St. Stephen, or rather with his Day, that it would be a bad day for a visitor to start his notes for a book about Ireland: such a book might start something like this: "The Irish people are very small, and mostly old and white-bearded; they have very long noses, and cheerful but devilish faces. Their clothes are of antique but varying fashions, and their complexions are either scarlet or dead white."

And all this would be the product of accurate observation; but no sooner would these notes be written than they would require to be amplified and amended. St. Stephen's Day would be distinctly a bad day on which to start a book about Ireland. For the wren, the king of all birds on St. Stephen's Day, was caught in the furze. And in order to celebrate this event Ireland rises upon this day in bands, mostly youthful and all

disguised, which go from house to house to pro-
claim the traditional truth that I have just divulged
to the reader. As I write there is a rhythmic boom-
ing of boots upon stone, which tells me that a
dozen or twenty men with strange faces, and even
stranger whiskers, who have just danced before me,
and danced extremely well, are dancing now in the
servants' hall. And this will go on until late. They
are the third band that have appeared since dinner
alone, and are much larger than those that an ob-
servant tourist might have seen on the roads all
day; because the earlier bands are by now in bed.

When I see them dance my memory goes back to
dances that we used to have on every St. Patrick's
Day for all the people on this estate; dances I first
attended knowing only London ballrooms. I very
quickly realized the great difference between the
two, and that I must be skilfully piloted if I was
to take any part in these intricate and beautiful
dances. The Irish dances are still what they were,
and what they have been for ages, while London
apes the dances, if such they can be called, of the
African population of foreign cities. I hope that
the Irish people will preserve their old dances;
but a wave of sophistication is sweeping over the
world, and it is to be feared that a people that
have already taken to politics may also take to the
dances that go with jazz.

I had a long walk over the heather and pink

mosses, and by the edges of square pools, once cut
for turf, with green moss floating in them, and now
and then past patches of white grass growing in
water; I had a long way to go to get the wind right,
and most of the snipe that I saw got up while wind
and sun were wrong, and in addition to that they
were wild, as they sometimes are when they have
only just come in, on their quest of the worm that
the full moon lures to the surface; and I got no
more than six. It is a strange garden, the red bog,
and odd things grow there, but not all of them are
flowers for folk like us, for they seem somehow too
fungoid for our gardens and even far from our
world. I noticed beside a patch of heather, on
which I was sitting for lunch, a pale-green company of tiny flowers with bright scarlet heads, but,
lovely though they are, they have no name among
flowers, belonging to some order of life that gar-
deners do not recognize. And then there are the
great mosses, seeming to grow brightest wherever
they have beneath them the greatest depth of water
or slime.

I got home in time to find a man in the uniform
of a policeman, except that he wore the badges of
rank of a naval lieutenant and a few rows of brass
buttons; and another in green tailcoat and brown
breeches; and one in frockcoat and tall hat; and
others dressed as diversely. The band had come
to my door to dance and sing. And one of them,

who wore the kit and the general air of a black-guard on a race course, imitated songs of blackbirds and thrushes with astonishing skill.

I do not think that these bands any longer carry and exhibit a dead wren, as they used to: the bird used to be chased over the furze earlier in the day, until it was too tired to fly any further, when the boys would kill it and put its body in a match box, and go round with it singing their song in honor of the king of all birds. I wonder what they would do to the saint himself, if he should return one St. Stephen's Day and appear in Ireland. I think it would all depend on whether or not he had the right religion and politics.

XXV

A Ride to Leixlip

Of Sunday I have little to say, for Sunday is
rather a day of gossip in one's own house and in
those of one's friends; and the gossip of my friends
belongs to them, even where they have permitted
me to share it, and is not a matter for print, and for
sale between covers. And Monday has come and
the full moon with it, and I walked the whole
length of a red bog, with the wind about right.
But there was something wrong with the red bog,
which my gamekeeper put down to the festivities
of the season, but which I think can be accounted
for quite as well by a frost that there was overnight; but, whichever it was, most of the snipe
had been either scared or frozen out of the red
bog, and I got no more than four.

But it is always pleasant, although not easy, to
walk in this wild and rather unearthly garden.
About half of our walk was on the low bog, that
had been cut away during the ages, and where the
pink mosses, like huge land-sponges, were slightly
in excess of the heather; and then we came to the
high bog, climbing up the soft brown precipice
along the ledges of turf-cutters, where there was

rather more heather than moss. This ancient and undisturbed bog ended in a promontory, cut away at both sides, and this narrow portion was all traversed by cracks like those of earthquake, as though the bog, with vacillating mind, had thought to move against the turf-cutters, as bogs sometimes do, and overwhelm them and their works, and had quivered once or twice and then slept again. A golden plover sailed over it and a flock of curlews rose, but not many snipe.

At one end of the bog we met a man carrying turf in an ass-cart, but the snipe were probably used to him; and he naturally chose the drier places, and it was not he that had disturbed them. Then we came home, past many splendors of Norman architecture, and past fields growing more and more fertile as we came away from the West, till we came to the very center of the cattle-trade of these islands; but both it and the Norman mansions are in ruins.

The next day was the warmest that we have had this month, and I went to shoot another red bog; but there must have lurked at the back of the warm wind an icy adversary that defeated it somewhere in the wastes of the ether, for soon after nightfall the moon was glaring on frozen grass, and a smell of old leaves burning seemed to drift from a new quarter. I got the small bag of nine snipe and a rabbit, but if the frost lasts it may be more snipe than I will get for a while.

And when the next day came the frost was gone, for the strange new wind had brought rain with it and washed the frost away, but it was none the warmer for that. Our Ireland—I beg your pardon, My Ireland, for that is the subject about which I have agreed to write—is always cold without our southwest wind. I went back to the small marshes, which are rather a relief after walking the red bog, especially the one I was on yesterday, where every step sinks deep into mosses like huge pink sponges, and has to be pulled out again; but sport was bad today on the black bogs, for it is the season when schools are closed, and boys are abroad upon quests that no one grudges them.

On the next day I shot a couple of birds more interesting for their variety in the bag than for their edible value; not that they are not eaten, or I should not have shot them. It was a couple of curlews, birds by no means rare, but not so often shot, except along shores, on account of a certain knack that they have of avoiding sportsmen. And I am glad they have that knack, for their beautiful and wild cry when heard far off gives a certain romance to the distance, or a strangeness to night. I have only shot one other this year, and would never shoot many of them, even were the matter in my hands, whereas it mainly rests with the curlew.

And on this day I saw what is nowhere so common as to be unworthy of mention, and is so beautiful that one should remember it, even if one did not record it, though it happened every day, and that is a kingfisher flying along a stream. He was an inch or two above the surface of the water along a stream that flows into the Boyne, and his blue, like the blue of skies shining over some southern story, too bright for reality, gave a sudden flash to the stream running under a winter's evening. He flew up the stream and came to his nest in the bank; and, though the brood will be hatched before this book is in print, I will not say any more of his lovely flight, for I would do nothing to give the least clue as to where his nest may be.

Then I passed some countrymen, with exactly that look in their faces that tells of the hunt being near; but I think it passed just out of sight. Two days ago the enemy of us all, or at any rate of our chickens, passed in full sight of my windows. It is time that the hounds met here. And now I am in front of my fire of turf again, thinking of former hunts.

My memory returns to the great hunt that we had on March 12th, 1904. By the following month the hind that we hunted then had come to live in my woods; and I went out to look for her with my harriers. After hunting up and down for a while she went away and, taking roughly the old line,

made for the Boyne, by whose banks I lost her after
a point of eight miles. On April 22nd, I tried
again, but could not find her. Nearly a year
passed, and on March 4th, 1905, the Wards came
to look for her in my woods. The hind by then
had been named after this place, in whose woods
she liked to live, and was known to everybody as
Miss Dunsany. They found at once and hunted
up and down my wood, then to another covert of
mine and then to two neighbors and back again,
when suddenly Miss Dunsany went straight away
southwards.

As we galloped south we came now and then
upon fox-coverts that we knew, which served at
first to tell us where we were. And then we came
to country that I did not know at all. And suddenly there was a town before me and I asked its
name and was told Leixlip, a town in another
county. It was a great moment, seeing that town
and hearing its name. We had done a point of
thirteen miles, and had been two hours and twenty
minutes over it, and on this rare occasion Miss
Dunsany was taken. I rode home by starlight, on
a horse that I had not often hunted and had not yet
named; that day I named him Leixlip, and he
carried me well in many hunts up to the end of
1912. I think that that is a good way to name a
horse, for it preserves good memories, and mem-

ories in which the horse deserves well to have his share.

I named another horse later in the same way, from a good hunt that started from a covert of mine called the Hill of Glane, the same covert from which Miss Dunsany went when she left the wooded land and went away to County Kildare; but on this occasion I named the horse from the hither end of the run and called him Glane. We had had the Meath Hunt ball at my house the night before and the woods near the house were blank, the foxes probably having had the sense to know from the smell of gasoline and various noises pretty much what was going on. The Hill of Glane, however, held a fox, and soon we were leaving the view to the north and west behind us and riding through smaller fields away from the high ground, till we came to boggy land, and a stream called the Derrypatrick river. Jumping the Derrypatrick river and crossing more boggy land, we came to larch-woods and checked.

It was a good hunt up to Culmullen, which was where we were now; but the Hill of Glane was the end of the hunt as well as the beginning, for, when the fox was viewed away from Culmullen, he went straight back again, and we hunted him back, though not so fast as we had come, over the old line of fences, through wider gaps, and so came back to Glane. A year later we had the ideal morning after a hunt ball, for we found at once in a wood near the house, and, riding practically from the door of the ballroom, went over the Hill of Glane, straight through the covert, and, taking just the same line as the year before, we came to the same small fields; and, remembering some particularly difficult fences that lay to the right, I kept to the left this time and found the going better, although there was much jumping.

We came to a house built on a mearing fence, which seemed to have no approach whatever from our side, as though it had no intercourse with anyone to the north of it. When we got round this house the fences were easier, though I had one fall. And we left the house behind us and came again to the boggy land, and to the Derrypatrick river, which we forded this time. And instead of stopping at Culmullen or turning back, he went straight on, and we came to country I did not know so well. Then I let the horse canter very slow for a while, as he had been a bit blown by his fall. And so I got him to the end of the hunt, though he fell again at the last fence; and a real good hunt it was.

Soon the Dunsany outlier, as she became from this on, was enlarged again by the Ward and I saw another good hunt. This was at the end of March, 1905. And on the 17th of April, I was looking for her in one of my woods with my harriers, and found her and hunted her up and down a bit and then she went away eastwards, and we had a good hunt for an hour and five minutes; and, like many others, we were unable to take her.

Back she came again to my wood the same evening, which she usually did when hunted; and the country people got quite used to seeing her trotting home here after a hunt; and they came to have a pride in her ability to outwit men and hounds, and used to say that she would never be taken. Five days later I hunted her again. And this time she took the old line to the Boyne, and after fifty minutes without a check we left her out beyond Trim, and, as my hunting diary records, took hounds home to rest for the summer.

I saw three more hunts with the Ward after the famous outlier; and Mr. Percy Maynard, the master of the Ward, promised to give me her head whenever she died. And some few years went by, and a cavalry regiment at the Curragh that had a pack of harriers found her and hunted her in County Kildare; and the great curse of a hunting country, which is barbed wire, was too much for her, and she ran into some and was badly injured and killed; and the master of the harriers sent her head to a Dublin taxidermist to be set up.

I had almost forgotten Percy Maynard's promise, but he had not; and he went into the taxidermist's shop and, bothering more about his promise than any legal rights, got hold of the head and sent it to me. And here it hangs on a wall, in the house where I write; it is crowded out by better-looking heads and hangs where few see it; it is getting old too, and was rather torn by wire when first it arrived; and to few of those that do see it does its name on an ivory plaque convey anything now. Once hundreds of men and women rode hundreds of miles behind that head, when it bobbed over Meath and as far as Kildare. It helps to keep bright memories from quite fading away, and sinking among dead thoughts; and soon the moth in the fur, and time among the old memories, will sweep head and remembrance away.

XXVI

Diving with the Ward

ONE must not write of hunting in Ireland without any mention of the culminating rite that brings all fox-hunters together, which is the Hunt Ball. There you will see every member of the Hunt; and not to be present then, if you belong to the Hunt, is to be thought dead. On such occasions the light-blue facings of the Meath may be seen varied by the white facings of their neighbors the Kildare, the French-gray facings of their northern neighbors the Louth, and the black collar and white facings of the Westmeath, with the single fox on the left lapel; all these facings, of course, on red coats. And if anyone ask a member of the Westmeath why his lapels do not match, or whether he has lost a badge, he or she will find the answer lurking, all ready to leap out, that the Westmeath only hunt one fox at a time.

The brilliant green facings of the United, from Cork, are likely to be seen too, and one or two hunt coats each from perhaps twenty different packs from anywhere in England or Ireland. At about midnight comes supper; and in the small hours, not before stars are almost beginning to pale, the bright gathering dances to the ritual tune of the fox-hunter, "Do ye ken John Peel." After that the National Anthem, and loyal fox-hunters singing "God Save the King" as well as they can, and then a few who-whoops, that should surely warn the foxes in coverts all round that for the next few hours their coverts had better be blank; and the sound of motors troubles the night, and gasoline mixes with the vapors of dawn.

The meet next morning is usually at twelve, instead of eleven, so as to give some chance of getting two or three hours' sleep; and nothing is more pleasant then than a run from the first covert, to bring the wind of the morning into eyes still a little sleepy.

Younger men will hardly believe me when I tell them that up to a few years ago there were men who were able to dance at a Hunt ball with no more stimulants or narcotics than perhaps a couple of glasses of champagne at supper and a single cigarette.

As much as the facings of the hunt-coats vary, so varies the country that the different packs hunt. Louth to the north of us, on the other side of the Boyne, is full of little hills, sometimes with gorse-coverts on the top of them and often with glimpses of the sea, like a dazzling frame round a picture. Then comes Meath, with its big fields and great blackthorn hedges, which I used to think were our principal hindrances to hunting, when they rose to twenty feet high along the deep ditches, and had few gaps in them; but of late years they have been very much cut. Those big fields, so splendid for galloping, are being cut up too; but the good turf remains, and the only real enemy is wire. We have very few hills like those of Louth, except at the north of the county; and in Ireland little hills and lakes seem to begin as you turn northwards from Leinster. Our neighbor on the south is Kildare, our principal rival, so that it used to be said, with the names of the hunts in varying order according to who told the story, that Kildare men might be heard saying: "Show me a Meath man till I lep on him."

The great plains of Kildare are as good for riding as the big fields of Meath: the ditches of Kildare are, I think, not quite so cavernous as ours, and I used to notice more narrow-banks in Kildare; in fact I hardly knew them until I met them there; though now they are building them fast in Meath. The great occasion of the Kildare hunt is Punchestown races, which we do not pretend quite to equal with any races we have in Meath. Between Meath and Kildare, and extending far into both, lies the country of the Ward Staghounds. These have some of the finest of the Meath country to hunt over, and some of the very deepest ditches; in fact I do not know of any very much deeper than those about the Bush Farm, near Fairyhouse.

Once hunting there with the Ward I got into one of these ditches, and I distinctly remember the water darkening as I went down. I hit the bottom and rose again to the surface, and my impression that this had taken some time was corroborated by an Irish judge on the top of the bank who told me that he was just about to get off his horse to go to my assistance, when he saw one of my hands come up. The job of getting my horse out, of course, took a good deal longer than it did to climb out myself. One should note that this was not a river, but just an ordinary ditch; and we have many like them in Meath. This is the country in which often in spring, and indeed before one had thought that winter was over, one comes on the sudden flash of patches of crocuses, mauve and orange and white, as one gallops past small lawns when the hunt is heading for Dublin.

Fairyhouse is the Mecca of the Ward Hunt. There they all meet on Easter Monday and have their famous races, and soon after that they have their last meet of the season, sometimes over a country strewn with the bottles and orange-peel of the day before. I have never ridden that course on a race-day, but I once rode it with the Meath, when we killed a fox in front of the Grand Stand. If there had been one prophet living in all Ireland,

I should think those seats could have been filled at
a good price.

The Ward are hard riders, many of them out
from Dublin for their one day's hunting in the
week, or at the most two, for the Ward only hunt
on Wednesdays and Saturdays, and the gallop just
after the hounds have been laid on, for its close
ranks and its casualties, has sometimes the look of
a cavalry charge.

Another neighbor of this country is Wicklow,
but beautiful though its mountains are, brooding
like sleepy giants over the sea, and its many fine
demesnes, it has not the perfect pastures of Meath
and Kildare, and the hunting of this county is done
by harriers. To the west of us the glorious quest
of the fox's brush is taken up by the Westmeath,
which has not our wide green fields, and it is there
that one begins to get the hint that Ireland is
mainly made of different soil from that of other
countries, and one sees the beginnings of that great
bog that, with few interruptions, goes bright with
heather and mosses westwards to Galway, the country of loose stone walls, where the Galway Blazers
have to hunt their fox along the edges of bogs and
do what they can to stop him from crossing unride-
able country, a country too that struck me when
first I saw it as having more fine castles than any
other county I knew, but all in ruins, as though
some great people had assailed the bog with their

culture and tried hard to plant it there, and the bog had won.

North of this line from Westmeath to Galway, foxes have a better chance of eating their poultry undisturbed; but south lie many good pastures and many good packs, King's County for instance, hunted by the Ormond, whose gorse coverts on hills I remember, and loose stone walls, and whose Master told me once that for some years he had managed, with the help of a pack of beagles which he took out on Sundays, to hunt seven days a week. And south of this lies the good Kilkenny country, where they have stony narrow-banks, as well as stone walls, and besides the Kilkenny Hunt there used to be a pack of harriers at Bessborough in this county; but they have burnt Bessborough.

And their neighbors are the Tipperary, a county with good pasture for galloping, except where the bogs begin, and with ranges of hills frowning down on it, and sometimes big woods. But if I followed that elusive creature the fox in imagination all over Ireland, there would be no end to it, for the pursuit of him in one county alone can be, and often is, the occupation of a lifetime, and foxhunting in my opinion deserves a place, with the graver more serious professions, among the great illusions of man.

XXVII

Magic

I was shooting coverts today, for the wind has
shifted round to the west, or even a bit to the north
of it, and the woodcock might be coming into the
woods, though the snow that drives them there has
not yet come. As I stood by the side of one covert
a robin came up to look at me, and I looked at the
robin, and we each seemed to be quite friendly to
one another; and then the thought occurred to me:
what will the robin think of me if he sees me kill a
woodcock? It may seem a trivial matter to record
in a book; and yet the elements of it are like this:
supposing you were dining with a lady in a restau-
rant, who did not know you very well but who
seemed to like you, and supposing you suddenly
beat in the skull of a waiter with a bottle and he
fell dead at her feet; might not you lose the lady's
confidence? I felt like that about the robin. But
when the woodcock did come I forgot about the
robin altogether, so that I cannot say what that
bird thought of it.

With pheasants and woodcock and pigeons today's bag has varied the larder, in which snipe
were too predominant, though I got a widgeon the

other day. Widgeon are rare so far inland as this, except by the lakes; though we sometimes hear their whistle along the Boyne, and it was on the Boyne that I got him.

When I came in from shooting today to lunch indoors, which I do when shooting the woods, we had lunch at one forty-five instead of our usual one-thirty; and just after one-thirty I heard a very indignant caw from a rook under the window, that was quite obviously a protest against the lateness of lunch, a matter that he was interested in because, in very hard weather, we used to throw out food for the birds, and it became a habit, and the rooks, who probably need it least, set the most store by it and after them the jackdaws. In rather the same way, if anyone's child is sick, and one gives it milk from the larder, or one's grandfather did in his time, the child will still get the milk every day, long after its beard is white; and, if the custom is not stopped then, it becomes a right in the child's family. And I've known the same thing happen with medicine.

And medicine suggests, though doctors might deny any connection, the strange cures that certain men throughout Ireland have for various maladies, old prescriptions handed down a long time in their families, and compounded of herbs. And some are made of stranger things, such as the fat of eels, that the wizard roasts in the patient's presence. Some

THE GIANT'S CAUSEWAY, MOST FAMOUS OF NATURE'S WONDERS IN NORTHERN IRELAND

BALLYSHANNON, SEAPORT OF COUNTY DONEGAL

of these cures depend upon faith, firmly grounded in magic, others on the genuine beneficence of herbs.

For a moment once I thought that some of the better ones, of which I had heard, ought to be put on the market and widely sold. But reflection taught me that a man who cured twenty patients or so in a year could not make the medicine for a million or so; and, when advertisement had made the demand, the supply would be manufactured by other hands and of other ingredients; and a blinder and stronger faith than the one engendered by watching the stewing of eels would mislead millions into supposing that the stuff was doing them good, and would enrich men far from Ireland. Let no man who believes in the hoardings, till he is angry if anyone doubts them, dare to deride the man who stews eels in front of his patient and uses their fat to cure deafness.

Wise men, wise women, holy stones, the drip of water on tombs, and much more besides, provide the magic that effects the cures. Some years ago there was a flare-up in the reputation of some holy stones about eighty miles from here; and the husband of a woman so crippled with rheumatism that she could not turn over in bed without friends to turn her, asked for the loan of my motor to take her to the holy stones to be cured. A hundred and sixty miles in a motor for such a case seemed haz-

ardous; yet, when a hopeless case suddenly has a
strong hope, one thinks twice before crushing it,
and I lent the motor.

It was a lonely scene at the holy stones, as I
heard of it: no one was there but one policeman,
with his hand on a holy stone. And it was one of
the times when they were shooting policemen. The
conclusion of this story is only hearsay, but I heard
that when the woman came back she was walking
about the house. Yet the power of the holy stones
waned in a few days, or the woman's faith weak-
ened, or the rheumatism was too strong; certainly
there was a relapse.

Holy wells do good work in this country too.
There is one not a mile from my door. And a
neighbor, when I was young, or a little before my
time, was traveling in the Holy Land, and lost his
hunting-crop there. I have often heard the story.
And I think he prayed to St. John, whose well it is,
for the return of his hunting-crop. But, at any
rate, he came home and found his hunting-crop
lying at the bottom of the holy well. Being an
educated man he made the mistake, as it seems to
me, of explaining the miracle, his view being that
there must have been an underground current running from Palestine into this part of County Meath,
along which his hunting-crop must have drifted.
I think that this was a mistake, because we cannot
say what a miracle might or might not be able to

do; but we can say, as definitely as we can say anything about geology, that the river under the Irish
Sea, and a few other seas, is impossible. In any case
why should a miracle be taken away from St. John
and thrown on to the back of Science, even if
Science were able to carry it?

And then there are stones that work curses instead of cures, of which I think the Blarney Stone
is the worst. For the kissing of that stone will
make you a rhetorician; and, when one thinks of
all the harm done by political speeches, one must
regard the stone as being among those many cases
in which Man gets no good in the end by any traffic
with magic.

Lest any who may credit me with an imagination
should think I am using it here, let me say that it
is all the other way about; for the country is full
of mystery and abounding in tales of magic, and
the people are inclined to be secretive even to those
to whom they are friendly, and I do not know one
in a hundred of the tales of magic they tell; and
those to whom they are not very friendly would
never hear one at all. And, were my imagination
not always kept on its chain by reason, I could tell
a very magical tale myself. But reason says it was
only a strange coincidence.

The facts of the tale are these: I had been working on a book called *The King of Elfland's Daughter,* and I had just finished a long chapter, in which

all the chief characters were will-o'-the-wisps. I
had described them rising out of a bog at night,
and told what they did. And that night I went to
sit for geese out in the middle of a bog not far from
here. And the will-o'-the-wisps came to me. I
saw them there for the first time in my life; but I
did not imagine that they had come to call on me,
lured by my long thoughts of them. The bog was
frozen and my footsteps had gone through the ice,
so that gases from the decay of age-old reeds had
no way out except through those holes made by my
boots. Consequently they were a thousand times
more concentrated than when they could rise from
the whole of the bog's surface; and, if ever they
were to shine, they shone then. A herd who lived
half a mile away on the dry land was waiting for
me at the edge of the bog when I came out by
starlight, and I asked him about the lights, which
he also had seen. It might be some kind of a flare,
he thought, lit by some man to find his way.

"But what would he be doing out on the bog at
that hour?" I asked.

And he had no answer to that.

"Mustn't it be a will-o'-the-wisp?" I said.

"Ah, I don't believe in Jack-o'-Lanterns," he
answered very quickly.

For he was afraid of the lore of his youth, while
his contemporaries were clutching at new-fangled
ideas. He thought that a Jack-o'-Lantern was a
leaping imp, carrying a lantern over the bog, but

that he ought not to believe in him. When he saw that I did believe in will-o'-the-wisps, he forsook them no longer.

"They do be all over the bog," he said; "and in spring it's terrible."

Yesterday I went some way to the northeast, looking for golden plover, till I was not far from the sea; and all of a sudden I saw them going over, but high out of shot and looking small like snipe. I stopped the car to watch them, and just there by the roadside was a thatched cottage I knew; and the dog that looked after the house seemed to remember me, though I had forgotten the dog; and he came up to me very friendly. And then I saw that it had lost one eye, and that the socket was in a terribly bad condition. The man who lived in the cottage was a friend of mine, and I felt that I knew him well enough to interfere on behalf of his dog. So I went and knocked at the door, the dog coming with me, and the man came out to greet me, and I asked him if he would take the dog to a vet; which he promised to do.

"How did it happen?" I asked.

"Sure, a man hit him in the eye with a whip," he answered. "And then, when the eye wasn't getting any better, Paddy poured some Lysol into it."

"Was Lysol a good thing to put in the dog's eye?" I asked.

"Seemingly not," he said.

XXVIII

Cricket

ONE field of mine, in between two woods, has always a lonely look to me, especially at evening; most of all on a fine summer's evening with the sun still in the sky. For it is a cricket-field, and the late light of warm days always reminds me of old cricket-matches, when the excitement was increasing with every over and the umpires would soon draw stumps. Here, since the later years of the last century, we used to play cricket through most of August and into September, against the cricket teams of cavalry regiments from the Curragh and battalions quartered in Dublin, as well as the Free Foresters, the M.C.C. and other English teams, and the Shulers, the Irish equivalent of the Zingari, and many other Irish teams. With the exception of the war we played cricket there right up to the time when Parliament passed what they called the Treaty, and the resultant troubles made the roads too difficult and uncertain for me to be able to collect a team.

During those years all the principal cricketers of Ireland played cricket on that ground, and it looks lonely without them. David Trotter, who

played for the Gentlemen of England when they
were captained by W. G. Grace, made many centuries here; and Bob Fowler, whose defeat of
Harrow in 1910 made one of the most sensational
finishes ever seen at Lords, played regularly for
me for many years: I do not think I ever saw a
bowler who could catch a ball as near to the bats-
man as he could; it was almost unsafe to play back
to him. And there were many splendid players
whose names would not convey anything to anyone
outside Ireland; such as Dr. O'Keeffe, who played
regularly for me, and who once when the opposing
wicket-keeper had an eyebrow laid open, not only
bound up his head for him, but took his place as
substitute at the wicket, being one of the two best
wicket-keepers in Ireland.

And then there was a friend who used once to
play football for Ireland, and was equally good
at cricket. I used to think that, whenever he talked
Irish politics, his hair stood on end and turned red,
but I fancy now that I must have been mistaken.
Bowling on the damper Irish wicket, some of those
who played cricket for me were able to get work
on the ball that sometimes surprised more experi-
enced English cricketers. One often played all
the week, including Sundays; but on Sundays it
was village cricket, cricket played by workmen
who had no other day on which to play it. There
was a school of thought in those days that held that

cricket was a form of slavery inflicted on free men by a bloody tyrant, but this view was not so widely held as to prevent one easily finding twenty-two men to play on Sundays, and a much greater number to watch and have tea in the tent. And they played it well and enjoyed it. Only occasionally, if there happened to be a political meeting at Tara, people cycling along the road to Tara, that passes our cricket-ground, might occasionally shout some remark such as a free man might throw at a slave who might appear to him to be deliberately wallowing in his ignominy; but this rarely occurred, and never detracted from the enjoyment of cricket.

When the chains were smitten off the wrists of Erin (I speak metaphorically and it is the usual way to speak of these things) some of the stigma was taken from cricket, and League matches were played extensively through the county. There may be some who, while expecting Irish political thought to be complicated, may not have supposed that such complications could ever be brought into cricket. For their instruction or amusement I will quote a problem that was brought to me as president of the County Meath Cricket League. The problem was this: the rules of the M.C.C. state that a bowler must have one foot behind the bowling crease. But the committee had detected a man who bowled with both feet behind the crease. This was clearly a breach of the rule, laid down in black

and white; and the committee were unanimous
about it, but appealed to me for the final decision.
Every now and then you will find perverse men
who go flat against the opinion of all around them;
and on this occasion I was one of them. Many
similar problems arise from time to time; and I
hope that cricket may survive them. And I hope
that they will not develop up to a certain point;
but I am afraid that, if they do, the M.C.C. will
be declared a heretical sect.

I used to play also for the Shulers, who wander
about Ireland, and for County Meath, which used
to have a magnificent ground in Navan, now gone
like so much else; and for the Phoenix Park
Cricket Club, who have a rather small ground, nice
and easy to hit out of, beautifully situated under
the Dublin Mountains. I know no lovelier ground
on which to play cricket. I was playing cricket for
the Shulers on August 3rd, 1914. I was hospitably
put up for the night, as Shulers always are, and
next morning my hostess told a story which I think
will always remain in my memory. She said that
at midnight a policeman knocked at the door, asking to see her husband, a retired colonel, who was,
I think, a magistrate. She was a little alarmed at
first about a policeman coming at night, and even
feared, she said, that something might have happened to one of the animals up at the farm, but it

turned out that he had only come about general mobilization for the Great War.

A Shuler dressed for his dinner is rather a gorgeous sight, while on tour, a sight that the Treaty somehow seemed to stamp out, and Na Shuler seemed dead for a long time; but I was very glad to hear only a year ago that the old club was revived. May it see many centuries, both of runs and of years.

And there was an earlier club of wanderers that used to come here to play cricket against us, when I was home for my holidays from Eton. It was called the Bog of Allen, and they used to drive up on a coach, with two poles, each topped with a sod of turf from the bog, and with heather growing on the turf, and they used to plant the poles by the tents when they played, with rather the air of Romans setting up their eagles. Yells used to come from the coach as they arrived, as a demonstration of a certain wildness appropriate to the great Irish bog. They said that the Bog of Allen was a hundred miles long; so that there was probably no good cricketer in Ireland who was disqualified geographically from being a member of that team. I do not know if members of the Bog of Allen founded Na Shuler, but they seem quite a possible origin.

On this ground as well as on the County ground I often played against Colonel Leslie Rome, of the

XI Hussars, who was the fastest bowler I ever batted against. He died last year. And, when I remember how he played cricket, and indeed everyone else with whom I played in those not distant days, I feel that far better cricket was played in country matches then than is played now in test matches. We did not get so many runs, or bowl balls so hard to play; but Colonel Rome, who could easily have killed any man that he hit on the head, never attempted to. That is the essential difference between our cricket and the best cricket of today, if you use "best" in the sense of being the most skilful.

I only once knew Colonel Rome hit any man, and that was when he broke two ribs of our Meath "pro"; but he never tried for it, and on the contrary bowled nearly every ball to the off, so as to avoid any such accident, occasionally straying on to the wicket to scatter it. I have myself seen an English bowler at Lords aiming at a man's head in a test match, though he missed it by going too high. Our obscurer cricket was more sporting, was in fact better cricket.

A wind is raging tonight. And after getting a mixed bag in the morning and afternoon, I sat again for duck at the pond to which they flight. There came the moment, as it always does when sitting for duck, when it grew so dark and late that one wondered if they were coming at all. And

before they did come it was so dark that I was able
to leave my hiding-place and sit on the edge of the
pond. I sat facing the wind; so that, as they always
come in against it, they came over my shoulder
from behind, and I found I got a better view of
them that way, appearing black against a darkening sky, than any other way I have tried. Few
came tonight, but I managed to get five. By the
time two retrievers had gathered them it was quite
dark, and lights however far off looked cheerful
welcoming things. And now the cries in the great
voice of the wind seem stimulating to memory,
and to memories I am turning.

And the next memory that comes to me is one
from a room in this house that is still called the
Magistrate's Room, because it was to that room
that prisoners used to be brought by the police, to
be dealt with by my father and grandfather in their
capacity as magistrates. Memories come to me
from this room, because the gun-room lies beyond
it, so that it is to the Magistrate's Room that I
always return whenever I come in from shooting.
And this is the little tale of it that I remember:
two of the constabulary, armed with rifles, marched
in a prisoner, and when the constable had to sign
some paper relative to the man's crime, remarking
"hold that," he shoved his rifle into the prisoner's
hand before taking up the pen. I do not suppose
that this little tale will ever come to the eyes of any

English statesmen; they are too busy for that. And it is too late now, even if it did. So really there is no use in my recording it. Let any who please smile at that trustful constable, if they should find his simplicity funny enough to smile at, and if they should feel that they have the right to do so.

XXIX

Dublin

Yesterday I was turning over old memories; and today when I set out after snipe I had a glimpse of the Dublin Mountains again, smiling in pale sunlight, and the sight of them turned my memories towards Dublin, once the capital of Ireland. Approaching it from the north one may go by Castleknock and through the lovely Phoenix Park, that seems to flow to the very feet of the golden slopes of the mountains, and so one enters Dublin along the Liffey, with its granite embankment which seems to treasure the memory of an old splendor, that is gone from the houses beside it; or one may come in by Sackville Street, now given a new name, a street so congested and narrow that it was lately said to be necessary to remove Nelson's statue and pillar that still stand in the midst of it, in order to allow the carts to get by; or, for there are two ways of measuring anything in Ireland, according to your religion and politics, the widest street in the British Isles.

I give the two measurements because both are interesting, and I leave the reader to choose which he will accept, according to his religion and politics, or, if he is quite impartial, to go and see for himself. At the end by which one enters Sackville Street, coming from this direction, one comes first to a statue of Parnell and, graved on the pedestal, this sentence from one of his speeches, "No man can set a limit to the march of a nation." And the graven letters are gilded. I trust that should any-one ever chance to lend this book to a foreigner he will first cut out this page; for, should the above idea get loose in Europe, it would be almost sure to wreck its civilization. Going down Sackville Street and over the Liffey, and through Westmore-land Street between Trinity College and the old Parliament House, that is now the Bank of Ire-land, and then either up Grafton Street to Stephen's Green or along Nassau Street to the Kildare Street Club and Merrion Square, and on to Fitzwilliam Square, one passes all the way by houses finely built and beautifully decorated, that are evidences of the very high level of culture that is now gone.

Leinster House, once the town house of the Dukes of Leinster is, I think, as fine a private resi-dence as I have seen in any capital, at any rate in the British Isles. For the last century it has been a museum, and one of its wings was the club house and lecture hall of the Royal Dublin Society, founded by George II. When the Treaty was passed this building was taken by compulsory sale from the Royal Dublin Society and was used by the Irish Senate, the Royal Dublin Society retiring to Ball's Bridge, where they hold the Dublin Horse Show. How beautiful are those lines of the Irish poet, Oliver Goldsmith:

> The man recovered of the bite,
> The dog it was that died.

Those who miss the splendors of the Vice-regal box and the entry of the Lord Lieutenant in his carriage, and his drive round the ground with postilions, and all that these things brought in their train to Dublin, say that the Dublin Horse Show is a thing of the past, and even avoid the show ground, content with their memories of the days of Lord Dudley, and regretting that nothing like them will come again for a long while; but others say that the horses are as good as ever they were and the jumping in the ring as good to watch as any that ever was; and they are right.

And, after all, the principal object of going to a Horse Show should be to look at the horses; so why not do that and never mind what is lost? In the jumping ring, besides the water jump and the timber that one would find in all such show grounds, there are fences that are particularly indigenous, such as the stone wall, and the big bank of an Irish double. Last year four officers from four different cavalry regiments came over and competed in the jumping ring with an Irish team of four, and two or three foreign teams, and the result was as fine a display of jumping as one is likely to see anywhere in the British Isles. The Horse Show is not the only show held at Ball's Bridge by the Royal Dublin Society, for we exhibit cattle and sheep there too; but it is much the best known one.

There are in Dublin three theater companies; which, in order of their seniority, are the Abbey Theatre, the Gate Theatre, and the Longford Players. In a way the Gate Theatre might be called the child of the Abbey Theatre, and the Longford Players the child of the Gate; but the metaphor is a bad one, and one would better convey the relation between them by saying that the Longford Players were a heresy broken off from the Gate, as the Gate was heretical to the Abbey.

The Abbey, which is about as old as the century, derived its sustenance from the munificence of the late Miss Horniman. Others helped, but no one should speak of the Abbey without remembering her name, for without it there would have been no Abbey to speak of. Miss Horniman must have been not merely generous, but she must have seen with considerable insight the possibility of a new kind of drama arising far from cities, or at any rate free of the influence of cities, which was at that time gripping the drama very tightly. Supporting her vision materially, she endowed the Abbey, and that vision became a reality.

So much for the Abbey Theatre's material side; but the theater had not been going long, when there came to it an inspiration that gives it a place above the Gate Theatre or the Longford Players: this inspiration was Synge. His material was the talk of the Irish peasantry, and one does not have to examine his plays very closely to find three prominent ingredients: poetry; humor, rather grim; and satire. The first two of these are so inherent in the diction of the Irish people that one cannot at once distinguish between raw material and workmanship, as sometimes in jewelry the curve of a large pearl will be used untouched, by a jeweler, for the shape of a figure of which it forms a part. As for the satire, when first a Dublin audience saw Synge's *Playboy of the Western World,* instead of regarding satire as one of the spices in a work of art, they concentrated their attention on it and booed the play. It was rather as though you offered a plate of roast beef, with all necessary vegetables and condiments, to someone not quite familiar with them, and as though he started his meal on the mustard, and were sick.

But in course of time Irish audiences got over the bitter taste, and came to enjoy the play. This play was followed by *Riders to the Sea, The Shadow of the Glen,* and others; and, when we lost Synge in 1908, he had left dramatic work that blew fresh on the theater, as though someone in a scene

in a drawing-room comedy had opened the window
to air blowing fresh over cornfields. This breeze
affected to some extent the whole contemporary
theater, and, for the Abbey Theatre, remained an
inspiration; but too soon the inspiration wore a
groove, and the grim mood of Synge turned towards
sordidness, when his pen was in other hands; and
many subsequent plays were written, not only for
the Abbey, with Synge's material but without his
inspiration. This was forced on my attention some
ten years after Synge's death, when I saw a play in
a theater in Londonderry and was introduced afterwards to the manager; and, being more critical
than tactful, said something about the play being
"Synge and water." To which the manager answered: "Who is Synge?"

And talking of Northern Ireland I believe that
Kipling was Irish on his mother's side; and only
a few days ago I happened to be reading one of his
poems called "The Gift of the Sea." When telling
of the power of Synge to those who did not know
him I used nearly always to quote the great ending
to his *Riders to the Sea,* when the woman whose
last son is drowned, triumphantly says that the sea
can do no more harm to her now. And what should
I see, when I read Kipling's poem the other day,
but this, the second verse:

> But the mother laughed at all.
> "I have lost my man in the sea

And the child is dead. Be still," she said,
"What more can ye do to me?"

The very idea that makes the apex of Synge's
play! This poem was written before 1896. I do
not wish to belittle Synge because a single gem in
his jewelry was cut by another man. But I think
Kipling should have the credit of that particular
gem.

Although many subsequent writers have worked
the same mine as Synge, which is, as I have said,
the natural talk of the Irish peasant, I think that
Synge threw up most ore in each spadeful. And
this is the reason that I have chosen him as representative of the Irish playwrights of this century.
I used to think that Lady Gregory probably took
notes of amusing things that were actually said by
Irish people; and her plays had to me the appearance of containing large pieces of real conversation. But Synge seemed to me to be more in touch
with their thought. If I am right in this, then
their methods of workmanship would be exactly
opposite: Lady Gregory would hear some witty
remarks, and one would expect her to write a play
to contain them; whereas Synge, inspired by some
dramatic idea, would set out to make his play,
using the talk of the people to do it, much as an
architect would plan to build a house first, and
would afterwards buy bricks for the building of it.

The Abbey Theatre also turned out many fine actors, and if I choose one as representative of them, it will be Fred O'Donavan, partly because of his acting of a part more than twenty-six years ago which is very vivid in my memory yet. And Miss Sara Allgood and her sister, Miss Maire O'Neill, are two magnificent actresses.

I might devote many chapters to the other playwrights who wrote, and who still write, for the Abbey Theatre, for the Gate and the Longford Players, but this book has an even more serious purpose, which is to tell what Irish people really think of the government of Ireland by two new parliaments. The thought of this purpose comes over me sometimes suddenly like a shadow, and I realize now that this book is far on its way and that I must devote myself at once to the essential part of it. It almost troubles me to remember that Old Mickey has twice failed to give me the important information I sought from him; and, though I feel perfectly sure he will do it yet, I went over today to see that neighbor with whom I had already discussed the matter.

"What's the matter?" he said.

"It's about that book of mine," I replied.

"Can't you get on with it?" said he.

"You see, there's only one thing that will really matter to people who read it," I said; "and that is what I told you before."

"Yes, I know," he said. "What the people really think about it all."

"Yes, and you told me," I answered. "But I wish you'd let me quote you. It would save me a long journey to see that old fool Old Mickey, who won't speak unless he's sure that nobody's listening."

"No, you can't quote me," he said. "And it wouldn't be the least what they want if you did."

"They'll want to know the truth," I answered.

"That's the last thing they want," said he. "I'll tell you what they want, and you'd better give it to them."

"Well, some of them want one thing," I said, "and some another, according to what particular politics they are addicted to."

"Not at all," said he. "They both want the same. And you give it them as I tell you. The Irish have got what they wanted and clamored for. Won't they want you to make it out the finest thing in the world? Of course they will. They'd look like bloody fools otherwise. And the English gave them the Free State. If that was the cleverest thing that the English ever did, won't they want all the credit for it? And mind you I'm not saying that it wasn't. But if it should turn out to be the damnedest silliest thing they ever did in their lives, will they want you to be reminding them of that? It stands to reason they won't. They'd want you to help them to forget it; or leave them alone to do that for themselves. And if you can't leave them alone, just say that it was the cleverest thing ever done. But don't go and babble the truth to them: what would they want that for?"

XXX

A Conversation in London

ANOTHER day has come, making my memories
that much further off, and the north wind is blowing; and looking in the direction of the Dublin
Mountains, I saw a range of silvery clouds, slightly
gilded, all in the shape of mountains. I was motoring as I saw the shining range, and at first saw nothing solid amongst its peaks, and then at one end of
the gilded crags I saw the bulk of one earthly
mountain very dark: it was one of the Dublin
Mountains. How they have changed since yesterday! And later in the morning the north wind
pushed the shining clouds away, and I saw all the
mountains clearly. Their heads and shoulders
were still dark as night, but between them and the
earth were shining lines, and slopes of hazy silver.
  How they have changed! And if those mighty
elder children of Nature can change in Ireland
like that, how should one look for stability in the
moods of the people that play at their feet? Yet it
is one of these moods that I wish to tell of, the
political mood, and soon now I must go and find
it out from Old Mickey, and then close this book.
For I disagree entirely with my friend who said

that my readers will not want the truth. They
need not read the book, but, if they do, they will
want to know just what the people think about so
vital a thing as our new political system. And this
Old Mickey will tell me.

The ether has just been throbbing with the "Londonderry Air," played in Belfast. And suddenly,
after having written so many pages of this book, I
wonder if the very essence of Ireland might not be
found more surely in music than amongst all the
material things which I have lately been trying to
analyze. The "Londonderry Air" is very widely
known now, but there was a time when I heard it
very rarely; and all I knew of it was that Colonel
J. K. McClintock (peace to his ashes), who com-
manded one of the battalions of the Royal Inniskilling Fusiliers, had copied it down from a manu-
script preserved by an old Irish lady. It is one of
those airs of unknown origin, that drifted down the
ages through Irish valleys. There is a great yearning in it, and a crying out for something so beautiful, that it will not be found in this world; and the
ancient singer who made it seems to be mourning
with all his heart because it will not be found.

If Irishmen had a continent to play with, or even
any large country, they would soon lose that dream
and, instead of yearning for the inaccessible, be
content with the second best or the third best or
even with Tammany. But they are in a land re-

mote from the world's affairs, a land under clouds
so thick and so far away to the north that the
Romans called it winter. Their dreams have to
suffice them, just as gold might have to suffice men
in a land that had no copper. Green fields, castles,
politics and old stones, of which I have told in
these pages, are far from the real Ireland.

The real Ireland is a land of dreams. It is for
the sake of the dream that we send ministers to
Poland and Ruritania, for the sake of the dream
that we have a Minister of External Affairs, and
keep an army. And if we are not looking at the
stars as we walk, or looking for them at broad noon,
we are looking back over our shoulders at what has
gone ages since, and peering back even further
through the mist and the haze of Time, to see
bright and clear in the radiance that shines from
our vivid dreams the kings and the heroes of days
that never were. And that we shall part with last
of all. No nation shall take from us our myths
and our fables; no man shall prove that our demi-
gods did not live: we would as soon give up St.
Patrick as give up the snakes he expelled. And
why? Because St. Patrick was real, and can look
after himself.

But the Irish snakes never lived, and so they
need our support. They need it, and they shall
have it. In stone and on parchment and on whatever craftsmen can ornament, long snakes with

crocodiles' jaws make our favorite design. In England men are proud to protect the weak, but that is scarcely knightly enough for us: we protect the non-existent. While an Irishman lives to defend them no phoenix will die, no leprechaun, no fairy. And as for our ancient kings and the gods of old and the demi-gods, to them our allegiance goes out; and we are less likely to forsake one of them for anything modern, than for the discovery of some still older Irish demi-god. If a man's family has fought for James II, that stamps him politically; yet if he wishes to be taken seriously he must have some older leanings than that, and show an interest in kings and heroes who have a need of his interest, because, except for our singing of them and dreaming of them and arguing about them, they were never really there.

What colony has England ever founded like ours? America she may feebly instance. There is nothing in that: America was there already, and her people had merely·to set foot on it, and do a bit of fighting when they got there, to kill off its rightful owners. What is that compared to Hy Brasil, the continent in the Atlantic? That is one of our colonies. We not only discovered it, but we imagined it and invented it. If we want another victory besides the hundreds won by our demi-gods, we can sing of another tomorrow. And nothing that

historians can record of the deeds of any of you
can equal what our singers will say of ours.

Historians! What can they do? They need
material for their work, and can do nothing without it. Our singers can glorify us without our doing anything. And a finer tale they make than
any one of your histories. Let us sit and smoke our
pipes in front of our doors, and let singers tell of
our glories, and we will not envy Napoleon plant-
ing his fleur-de-lys on the walls of Troy, or wherever he did achieve his laborious victories. And in
any case what was he, only a foreigner?

I have written of our cattle trade being ruined,
and just as I am writing this I read today in the
Press that negotiations about it have been reopened
in London. The situation is well enough known
in Ireland, and I only write of it here for English
readers, who may not as yet quite have compre-
hended the subtleties of it. Semi-officially, then,
the negotiations are upon these lines: we owe to
England a sum of about five million pounds on account of certain land annuities, as has been ad-
mitted here. But to whom shall we pay the debt?
To the English? Certainly not. What are they,
only a lot of Angles, Jutes, Saxons and Danes, and
Normans? And what right had any of them—
that's what we want to know—what right had they
to come to England at all?

Look at the Danes! A lot of pilfering marauding massacring pirates. It was bad enough that all these foreigners got England, but for us to pay money to them, which is due to the land they stole, would only make matters worse. As for any promise on our part to pay, what about their own promises? What about Hengist and Horsa? There were a pair of Jutes! They were Jutes if ever there were any. And what did they do? They promised to help the rightful inhabitants of England against the Picts and the Scots. And they turned out to be just a common pair of land-grabbers; and they took most of England for themselves, a couple of Jutish foreigners. And are we going to keep promises to people like that? Let them keep their own promises first, let them give back England to its rightful owners.

The foreigner who called the English foreigners was righter than he knew. They are the most foreign lot of foreigners you could find anywhere, the scourings of Denmark, Jutland, Saxony and Normandy. Let them go back to the land of the Angles, from which they took their name. But they are so foreign that no one knows where it is, so that they must always remain foreigners wherever they are. Are we to keep promises to a people like that? And then there is the Poynings Act, which I have not read, but which has a great deal to do with it too.

This is merely the rough outline of what is today

being discussed in a hotel in London. Naturally it
cannot be got through in the few minutes in which
it takes to read what I have written about it. It
will probably take several weeks. These Jutes,
these pirates from Denmark, these Norman adven-
turers, have not yet understood our argument, and
have merely bluntly replied by putting a tariff
against our cattle in order to recover their debt.
But when they have come to see that they have no
rights in Ireland to recover any debt and that they
are only foreigners, having no *locus standi* anywhere, it is semi-officially said that it is thought in
well-informed quarters that something will soon
be done, unless, as may be the case, it should be
decided otherwise.

XXXI

Growing Oats in the Rain

AGAIN I saw the Dublin Mountains. I went to a funeral at Castleknock, and they were draped in rainy clouds as though they were mourning.

One might perhaps watch these mountains every day, noting all their changes that frown and smile through a year; and watching, or rather fancying, their variability reflected in the moods of the people that live on the plain below them. And it would not be only fancy, for of soil and climate are made the principal graving tools that shape the spirits of nations. Indeed I know of no other implements that Destiny employs for this purpose. So one might sit and watch those mountains and the storms that blow over them, and translate all one saw into the common thoughts of the people, and so write a better book about Ireland than I have been able to do, troubling myself with occasional facts. And the more one goes after figures and facts, the further, I believe, is one likely to get away from whatever one studies. For no large theme is capable of mathematical statement; so that the more precise the logic of one's summary, the shorter it must have fallen.

For two reasons I have not given the figures of the value of our exports and imports for last year; one is I do not know them, and the other is that, for the reason I have just stated, they do not seem to me worth while finding out. The number of pounds that we made or lost one year on the balance of exports and imports teaches us nothing: what will teach us something, if we can find it out, is the nature of the soil of the country, the crops or the cattle to which it is best adapted, the weather that will help it or trouble it, and the ability and the will of the people to work it. Neglect these principles, and a man in an office in a town will say: "Why are there not more oats? Let more oats be grown." And more oats will be sown, either in unfertile soil, like a bog, or in fertile soil, like the land of Meath.

Such errors may well be made by men who walk pavement. And the worst of the two errors is when the oats are planted in the fertile soil. For the ages have taught that Meath is the place for pasture. The Milesians knew that when they came to Tara, and everybody that has lived here since. But a townsman can scratch out the wisdom of the ages with a single stroke of his pen. We have planted oats here in Meath, of late, in the deep alluvial soil. And I have had the same report of them every year for the last ten. And it goes like this: "There was a wonderful crop of oats. The

BLACK ROCK CASTLE, WHICH ADDS PICTURESQUENESS TO THE HARBOR OF CORK

L. J. Heffernan—from Gendreau, New York

A MISTY MORNING IN THE TOWN OF KILLARNEY

finest I've seen. And if it hadn't been for the rain
that we had in August it would have been the best
crop ever seen anywhere. It was extraordinarily
bad luck. It came just at the wrong moment."

It was not back luck: it only came of ignoring
eternal things; and, in comparison with those who
ignore them, the gambler is wise who backs a horse
without having troubled to notice the more ephem-
eral matter, as to whether or not it is starting.
We need only have looked at our deep green grass
that luxuriates in our fields, to know that the rain
required to make it thrive like that would beat all
our oats flat. They should grow oats in England,
in the less fertile soil, and we should send them
cattle from Meath and Kildare. But to do that
would be tantamount to approving the action of
Hengist and Horsa, which we have proved to be
morally wrong. So we grow oats in the rain.

And don't let Englishmen be too critical of us
for our preoccupations. I have known some Englishmen get just as sodden on beer as we do upon
history. To sit and soak over anything is bad,
whether it is history, whisky or beer. But, I can
imagine an Englishman saying, our history is
mostly false. Well, so is their beer. If they put
chemicals into their beer, as they do, aren't we just
as much entitled to put in exciting events to ginger
up our history? The point is not that the stuff's
false, but that we sit and soak over it till we get

all fuddled and can't see what is really going on
in the world, and the Englishman frequently does
the same with his beer. So what right have they
to criticize us? Let any nation that has given up
all drink and drugs of every description criticize
us freely. But when that happens it will be on
account of the millennium, and we shall all be
living then in a perfect world, and we shall give
up our history and our politics, so that there will
be nothing for them to criticize.

But I was speaking of the three things upon
which our history most depends; the soil, the
weather, and the will of the people to work the
first with the aid of, or in spite of, the second. So
to this I will return. Our soil, in most of Leinster,
is deep and dark and fertile; the product of blue
limestone, that the ages have softened for us, or
of silt that old rivers have worn for us from the
rock and laid deep for our pastures. In this, nur-
tured by rain, the grass grows thick and tall, so that
I have seen fields of hay in Kent that had thinner
crops when they were fully grown, than our graz-
ing fields have in Meath. And the moisture that
gives our grass such easy growth gives a certain
ease to the people: it is not a climate against which
they have had to struggle.

Activity, in fact, may be looked for where it is
needed, in barren fields and on mountains, rather
than in rich pastures that thrive almost unaided by

man. It is from fertile eastern lands that the word
Kismet comes, which means that there must be no
struggle against Fate. The Arabs in their deserts
use the same word, but they must have borrowed
it, for they are a conquering people. In Ireland
we have the equivalent of Kismet, that negation of
struggle; and, however turbulent we may appear,
that phrase is in frequent use and lies deep in the
Irish spirit. "Ah, it's the will of God." The meaning and application of this phrase never varies; it
implies, whenever you hear it, that it is useless to
struggle against what has been ordained to come,
and is in fact the last word of resignation. It
means, for instance if a house has caught fire, that
the fire would never have come had not God willed
it; what, therefore, is the use of tearing down the
thatch to try and save it, when the house was ordained to burn, and must, therefore, burn whatever a man may do?

But the mild air that gives this ease and that
makes the soil fertile does not blow over soil so
easily fructified, in every part of Ireland. Yet still
that comfortable attitude endures, that easy ac-
ceptance of what Earth has to give to her children,
even in those parts of Ireland where Earth is a
poor mother. Perhaps the people recognize, with
some spiritual intuition, that the intention of our
southwest wind is friendly; for they see it making
even the rocks fertile, though with nothing more

useful to man than gorgeous mosses. Even our
stone walls yield their luxuriant crop, though only
of ferns, and our ruined towers grow ivy with the
ease with which fields grow grass.

Often in Meath or Kildare a field will dip to a
hollow, and there the rushes grow in the too-
abundant water that makes the bogs: as one goes
westwards those bogs increase, and soon one comes
to the borders of the red bogs, which do not pamper
man like the fields of Meath, and indeed give him
nothing except at the point of the spear-like spades
with which men cut the turf. And it does not
always even spare his life. Yet even here and
amongst the stony mountains the Irish people's
attitude is the same to the Irish earth, the happy-
go-lucky attitude of a spoiled child to its mother,
a child that knows that, whether that mother is in
poverty or well off, no harm will be allowed to
come near it.

XXXII

Farewell

AND now that my book is drawing so near to its
close, I feel I must go to Tara so as to close its
pages where I opened them when the pages were
yet blank. I will go at once. But it is a stormy
night, with a south wind full of rain, and I could
see nothing if I went there now. So I must go with
memory, and look with imagination. Shall I see it
clear tonight? There is something in the flames
going up from my fire of turf that makes me think
that I will. So let us go to Tara. Yes, there is the
view before me, lit with parish-wide pools of sunlight, and frowned on by shadows of clouds; while
between heaven and earth run hundreds of slanting
lines of interwoven sunlight and rain.

To my left hand, looking west, lie the Dublin
Mountains, that so seldom frown, smiling like
great benign idols of rather pale gold. Below
them out of sight lies Dublin, with its beautiful
Georgian houses, fallen on evil days; but though
Dublin is hidden from my eye standing on Tara,
my memories of it are vivid and clear, and these
memories seem to run and play more than anywhere else in the room where A. E. sat over his

dismal journal, while the fairies of his imagination that he had painted walked in elfin glades on the walls. Beyond the streets Dublin opens out into gracious suburbs, where pleasant demesnes run out to the feet of the Dublin Mountains.

So twenty miles away on my left the land is haunted by the memory of a master poet; while ten miles on my right lie the woods of Slane, crowning the hills that look on Slane Castle and the village of Slane, which are hidden, and the memory of an apprentice poet haunts these hills, Francis Ledwidge who died young, having given ample promise of being, in his different way, one day as great as A. E. And in their love of Ireland they were already equal. Behind those hills, like the rumor of some great army passing unseen, are a few gray lines, no more than the hints of mountains. And further away to the north, the Mournes rise up, communing with the sea.

Turning again to my left, and following the line of the Dublin Mountains, they dip unto green fields, and for a while there is no more distance in the scene, but familiar neighboring fields, fields that my harriers have gone over in old days in and out, and here and there small woods. Then distance appears again in that blue robe of hers, and the heads of the Slieve Bloom Mountains that are just too solid for clouds; and then the Hill of Usnagh alone by itself, with the hint of being

draped in blue velvet. Then right before me the
white spire of Trim, and after that, turning all the
while right-handed, mountains begin to appear,
roaming away northwest, so many of them that
imagination can scarcely number their company.

It is over there at the end of the long line of them
that kings that died on Tara were carried away to
be buried among carved stones, that tell their story
still, but in a language that none of us knows. The
pale golden ghosts of flames go flickering up from
my turf fire, as my imagination looks westwards
from Tara beyond the spire of Trim.

And now I realize that the time is come to set
down what, though it will come so late in this book,
is yet its main purpose, the matter on which I have
already approached Old Mickey twice. I must go
now westwards, passing south of Trim and all
through that blue distance, and find Old Mickey;
and this time, if anyone should be near enough to
trouble him with the risk of being overheard, I
shall merely wait till they are gone, though I
should have to wait all day.

The night blew wildly away, and a cold day
shone in its place, and as soon as I had had breakfast I set off in my car for Cranogue, to find Old
Mickey and to complete this story. Mountains as
I went lifted their gray heads over the horizon and
went down again; and, though I was traveling
towards them, for a long while I saw them no more.

I passed a gipsy encampment that was moving, with its bulging green wagons, its thin, tall men, dark women and keen-eyed children. They were separating as they started, one part going westwards, I think to Galway, probably carrying sheets of copper, to make stills to be set up in bogs far from dry land, to brew whisky by night; and the other party seemed heading straight for the border, to take the fullest advantage of it, now that the purely alien invention of Irish unity, forced on an unwilling people by the English, has left our shores with them.

It is a cold day full of rain that was lately snow, or that is hovering on the verge of change into that lovely substance, but my sympathies and my fancy left the comfort of my motor to follow awhile the wagons roaming the roads to the North. A boy of twelve following one of the wagons went by, whose bright and beady eyes I seem to remember having seen one day last year. We were each of us practising our art by the side of a lane; mine, that of a snipe-shooter; his, begging. He was coming along the road with his dark mother when a driven snipe went over, and I managed to hit it. "That's the finest shot I ever saw in my life," said the boy. Yet it was not my art that was so greatly excelling that day, but the art of the gipsy, the art of flattery neatly administered, like castor oil made tasty with spices. The wagons passed with that touch of romance that always seems to go with them, and the road was lonelier. Lonely, but bright and blue; for the sky was in its wet surface, as soon as the rainstorm passed. We came to wilder country, land where little bogs were more numerous, so numerous that people had to cross them on their way to and fro, and one caught glimpses of little passes made over the deeper bits by the trunks of birch-trees thrown down, or gorse, or anything that came handy.

The land was getting poorer as we went, and it seemed that there was a homelier look in the cottages and farmhouses than there is in the wealthier land, as though people fighting against bog and weeds and rock fought hard and had established themselves firmly: a sheet of corrugated iron will do for a roof in Meath where the soil would lavish wealth, were it not for our politicians; but in the harsher land that might starve them they seem to have built their citadels strong and to have raised their defenses of thatch to defy the weather. Large willows covered with ivy seemed to be stalking these lands, with great branches outstretched, giving to all the region an air of wildness, as though man's hold were uncertain, and Nature's more ancient children might take his place in the end. And the mountains came up again, less blue than when seen from Meath; and donkey carts passed us, rambling along the road, carrying loads of turf;

and the scent from the smoke of chimneys was the scent of its burning, unforgotten by all that have known it; and then the red bog appeared close by the road, and I knew that I was getting near to Cranogue and the house of Old Mickey.

I had brought ample provisions with me, for I was determined to wait however long might be necessary to find Old Mickey undisturbed. And then the white walls of Cranogue flashed into sight, and there was Old Mickey sitting before his door quietly smoking, and not another soul in sight. I stopped my car at once and got out there and then, and asked my chauffeur to go straight to Sharkey's Hotel, for I was determined that there should be nothing to interfere with Old Mickey's penchant for talking his politics privately. We greeted, and there was never a man in hearing.

And with every courtesy Old Mickey asked what had brought me. I explained, for he seemed at first to have forgotten the quest of information to which I attached such importance for the purposes, indeed the main purpose, of this book. And then it all came back to him; but he did not answer at once. He took his pipe from his mouth, and shook his head, looking grave. And the first words that Old Mickey spoke were not in answer to my inquiry.

"Did you hear tell of Mike O'Mahony?" he asked.

"I did not," I said.

I did not even know the man's name.

"He was shot," said Old Mickey.

"Shot!" said I. "How did it happen?"

"He was found in a ditch a bit west of here," said Old Mickey. "Aye, a bit to the southwest."

"But how did it happen " I asked again.

"Ah, wasn't he always a talker?" said Old Mickey.

"But what did he do?" I asked.

"Nothing—only talked," said Old Mickey. "Sure he was always talking."

"But how was he shot?" asked I.

"Ah, don't be wasting your sympathy on him," said Old Mickey, detecting some in my voice. "He brought it all on himself. Sure he never could keep his mouth shut."

"Poor devil," said I.

"Ah, what was he, only a Protestant? Not that anyone would think any the worse of him for that. Sure it's the grandest religion in the world; and no one would wish to hurt him on that account. Only, sure, a man with a religion like that ought to be careful, and not be abusing the people's tolerance."

"Who got him?" I asked. Not that the name of the man would have been likely to have conveyed anything to me, but only out of that politeness, that is I trust in all of us, and that makes us take at least

some passing interest in what is interesting the folk
with whom we may be.

But the question brought a dreamy look into Old
Mickey's face, and he looked thoughtfully up at
the sky and then shook his head.

"Sure I never had any memory for names," said
he.

Suddenly the fear came over me that Old Mickey
would fail me.

"The people like their new government, don't
they?" I blurted out rather too hastily.

But I could see by a far-away look in Old
Mickey's eyes that he was thinking still of the body
of Mike O'Mahony, to the southwest in a ditch.

"Always a talker," he said. "Aye, always a
talker."

And he closed his own lips, then, on the stem of
his pipe. And not another word could I get from
Old Mickey, except for his graceful farewells;
whose abundant courtesies seem more than what
one man can deserve, and which I would, therefore,
like to share with my readers.

Lightning Source UK Ltd.
Milton Keynes UK
UKOW04f1415160415

249766UK00001B/101/P